GET LUCKY!

MAKE YOUR OWN OPPORTUNITIES

GET LUCKY!

Make Your Own Opportunities

Theresa Cheung

Newleaf

Newleaf
an imprint of
Gill & Macmillan Ltd
Hume Avenue
Park West
Dublin 12
with associated companies throughout the world
www.gillmacmillan.ie

0 7171 3527 6
Print origination by O'K Graphic Design, Dublin
Printed by ColourBooks Ltd, Dublin

This book is typeset in Bembo 11/14pt.

The paper used in this book comes from the wood pulp of managed forests. For every tree felled, at least one tree is planted, thereby renewing natural resources.

A CIP catalogue record for this book is available from the British Library.

1 3 5 4 2

For Robert and Ruth

ACKNOWLEDGMENTS

I had my doubts about whether I had the credentials to write about luck. I'm not a lottery winner or a pop idol. I've never won any competition I've entered, or even got a prize in a raffle. However, the more I thought about what being lucky was, the more I realised that this didn't matter. If being lucky is about being happy, beating the odds, and achieving your dreams, then I am a very lucky person indeed.

A great deal of my good luck is due to the people who have helped and supported me.

I'd like to thank my publishers, Gill & Macmillan, in particular Michael Gill and Eveleen Coyle, for believing in me and giving me the opportunity to write this book.

Thank you to all the people who shared their good and bad luck stories with me and gave me an insight into how lucky people create opportunities. Names have been changed to preserve anonymity, but you know who you are. Thank you to Steven Covey, Azriela Jaffe, Phil McGraw, Aaron T. Beck, Norman Vincent Peale and Marc Myers for their excellent perspective on life.

Thanks also to Dr Priscilla Stuckey for her fine developmental editing and, for their support, to family and friends, especially my brother Terry and his partner, Robin.

And finally special thanks to Ray, my husband, for his love, support, patience and understanding and to my two gorgeous children, Robert and Ruth. I am indeed lucky to have you in my life.

Contents

Preface

Let's face it: lucky people fascinate us. The idea of someone who has found success or wealth with apparent ease and good luck by chance is irresistible, and it's hard not to sigh, 'If only!'

Yet chance and luck are two different things. Chance is random. Every day when you walk outside, anything can happen: you may bump into an old friend or be splashed by a passing car. Luck is different. Your luck depends on how you respond to chance and whether or not other people decide to help you get what you want.

'Some people have all the luck,' you hear others say. But have you ever thought why it is that some people manage to attract great opportunities when for others nothing seems to go right?

According to psychologists, it is because lucky people know how to attract good luck and make everyone want to help them get what they want. The secret doesn't lie in carrying a rabbit's foot. Creating good fortune for yourself is a skill and an attitude anyone can master. What truly sets lucky people apart is the way they behave. If you want to be lucky, all you need to do is start thinking and behaving lucky. This book will help you do that.

In part 1 you'll see that many of the people you think of as lucky are no different from you. They know how to make life go their way. In part 2 you'll discover the nine secrets of lucky people. Mastering these skills may not guarantee a lottery win or the leading role in a Hollywood blockbuster but they will help you become luckier than you are now. You'll find yourself attracting opportunities you might never have thought possible. Most important of all, you'll be a lot happier—and happy people are, after all, the luckiest people in the world.

From time immemorial people have wanted to know how to get luck and how to keep it, so in part 3 we'll look at some good luck charms and customs. I hope I've gathered enough good luck here to reassure you that wonderful things can and do happen if you live in hope and happiness and the expectation of them.

Get Lucky! was written not merely to be read but to be experienced. I hope you'll use the ideas in this book to help you attract good fortune in all areas of your life. Change can be frightening, because it involves risk; but if you are willing to try, to take a chance on change and follow the principles outlined here, there is no doubt you can become the lucky person you deserve to be.

The best of luck to you!

PART ONE

Introduction to Luck

'It is what a man does with his luck that makes it good or bad.'
(James A. Walker, *Nation's Business*)

1

MEET LADY LUCK

Lady Luck has been wooed and fretted over ever since humans lived in caves and learned to make fire. We will probably believe in her until the end of time, just as we have done from the beginning. Blessings and curses, fortunes changed in an instant, lives snatched from the brink—all fuel the idea that Lady Luck is a flirtatious and independent spirit. Yet, however badly she treats us, we continue to be fascinated by her.

From the young entrepreneur who banks his or her first million to the old-age pensioner reunited with lost loved ones, stories of amazing good luck never fail to intrigue and inspire us. Admit it, you're probably reading this book because lucky people fascinate you. How do some people manage to get what they want without appearing to work hard, you wonder. Is their good luck simply chance? A matter of good timing? Is it about talent? Or are they simply blessed?

Inspired by the apparent ease with which some people find success, you get impatient waiting for it to be your turn. But what if you didn't have to wait for good luck? What if there was a way to make your own luck?

Surely that's not possible, you say. Luck is one thing you can't control. But it is possible. Here is one amazing fact: instead of waiting for good luck to find you, you can create your own luck. Creating luck is a skill and an attitude towards life you can master. By making specific changes in your behaviour, you can attract more good luck.

This book will let you in on a simple yet life-changing secret. Lucky people aren't any different from the rest of us, except that they have one major advantage that sets them apart: they don't wait for good luck to find them. Instead, they learn to make their own good luck by taking positive steps to attract it. Later we'll explore the ways they go about doing that, but first we need to understand what luck is and what it isn't.

WHAT LUCK IS AND WHAT IT ISN'T

Isn't luck simply chance? Something over which you have no control? Luck just happens to the fortunate few for no apparent reason, right?

Wrong. Your first step to becoming lucky is to realise there is a huge difference between luck and chance. Let's take a closer look at the words *luck* and *chance*. You'll see that, although the words are closely related and chance is an ingredient of luck, they don't mean the same thing.

Webster's Dictionary describes chance as something that happens without an apparent or determinable cause or as the result of unpredictable forces. Chance describes random events—both big and small—that happen all the time. A rainstorm, the unpredictable bounce of a tennis ball, the shape of a cloud, a devastating earthquake, a black cat running across your path and similar unpredictable happenings are all chance. Sometimes there is nothing you can do to avoid misfortune and it is a matter of wrong place, wrong time, and unfortunate circumstances.

Luck is different. According to Webster's, luck is a force that brings good fortune or bad. You contribute to this force by how you react to the circumstances in your life. Good or bad luck is at least partly the result of your actions and behaviour in the world.

Creating luck often depends on the actions you take when confronted with a situation. You create good or bad luck by the way you respond to chance. We are both at the mercy of circumstances out of our control and capable of influencing our lives to a greater degree than most of us think. We live in a random world. We can't always choose what will happen to us, but we can control how we react, and that is what counts.

The Greek philosopher Epictetus offered this advice: 'Whenever chance befalls you, remember to ask yourself how you can turn it to use.' Life doesn't always happen as we would like it to. Uncertainty is a fact of life we all have to deal with. But lucky people know how to adapt to this environment of uncertainty, and that's what makes them winners. Lucky people know when to walk away from danger, how to recognise opportunities when they are presented to them, and how to get other people on their side.

YOU AND CHANCE

Take a moment to think how much chance affects you. Think of those chance meetings or events that became, in retrospect, turning-points in your life. Think about how your reaction to these occasions made all the difference. By chance you notice an ad for a job that changes your life. What if you had not bothered to apply? By chance you sit with strangers in a train who become good friends. What if you had decided to bury your head in the paper and not strike up a conversation? By chance you take refuge from the rain in a café and meet the love of your life. What if you had remembered your umbrella?

Think of chance occurrences as being the seeds of luck. A coincidental meeting, a chance remark, a sudden encounter, something you happen to read in a book could all trigger a series of lucky events. Chance crosses our paths all the time, but it is how we respond that matters. At any moment you might meet a person or have an experience that could transform your life for ever.

There are a number of ways to respond to a chance event, and you create your luck by seizing the moment. You are the one who has the power to transform chance into good or bad luck.

It's chance that you saw this book and decided to read it. How you respond to the information it contains could change your life. Whether it does or not is up to you.

Exploring luck

Before we explore in more detail the idea that luck is something you make, let's find out a little more about this mysterious lady. Where did the word *luck* come from? What do most of us think of when we talk about luck? Can ideas that attempt to explain luck actually improve your luck?

As far as we know, the first use of the word *luck* dates from the thirteenth century, when it entered the Middle Dutch language as *luk*. The *Oxford Dictionary* says the word probably began as a gambling term. Whatever its origin, it made its way across to England, where it turned up in Shakespeare's *Merry Wives of Windsor* ('Good luck lies in odd numbers . . . They say there is a divinity in odd numbers, either in nativity, chance or death'), in George Meriton's *Yorkshire Dialogues* in 1693, and in Jonathan Swift's *Polite Conversations* in 1738.

In 1654 a distinguished Frenchman called Antoine Gombauld Chevalier de Mere, Sieur de Baussay, developed what we think of today as probability therapy—the technique of weighing the odds to determine the most likely outcome. And so, in the highly fashionable but slightly disreputable atmosphere of the gambling rooms, and announced in letters of French gentlemen of the seventeenth century, Lady Luck was born. How the noun *luck* became the adjective *lucky* is unknown, but from the middle of the nineteenth century *lucky* can be found in print and almost always in relation to people with a knack for gambling.

Gambling

> Games of chance are as old as the gods themselves, according to the Ancient Greeks. On Mount Olympus, that realm of deities, an affair between the chief god, Zeus, and Tyche, goddess of fortune, produced a daughter, whom they named

> Gaming. From her tenderest years she delighted in inventing games of chance and watching the chaos and discord that resulted. Despite this, Gaming was fascinating and had many admirers. Her mother lit her daughter's palace with bright lights that burned all night, and Gaming was never without company. According to some accounts she gave birth to twin sons, Duelling and Suicide, who followed her guests to the door of the pleasure palace as they left—grim company indeed for those who followed Gaming's wanton ways.

Mention the word *luck* and gambling immediately springs to mind. In its crudest interpretation, gambling means trying to get something of value by risking the loss of something else. Luck is the very life-blood of the gambling capital of the world, Las Vegas, where fortunes are won or lost by the toss of a dice or the turn of a card. Gamblers flock to Las Vegas by the millions, all vying for the smile of that fickle queen who reigns supreme, Lady Luck.

As one of the oldest types of human behaviour, gambling has fascinated people down the ages, because it appeals to two basic instincts: greed and the thrill of uncertainty. The possibility of instant wealth sends planeloads of people to Las Vegas—the city that never sleeps—and tempts millions of us to buy lottery tickets. But Lady Luck is capricious by nature. Fortunes can be reversed in an instant, not just in gambling but in life itself.

To a greater degree than many of us would like to admit, we don't have complete control over our lives, and we are at the mercy of chance. Life is a gamble. We live in a world of uncertainty—sometimes for good, sometimes for bad. We are all the victims of misfortune from time to time, and we say, 'That's the luck of the draw.'

Sometimes there is a colossal strike of misfortune. The nightmare of 11 September 2001 is etched for ever in people's memories. Every day we hear of uncontrollable disasters: a tornado sweeps through a town, an earthquake devastates a city, the stock markets plummet. Bad things do happen to good people. It isn't fair and it isn't right, but for some unfathomable reason it happens.

You can take steps to limit the amount of risk you are exposed to, but you can't escape chance altogether. Finding the cruel uncertainty of life too daunting, some of us don't take risks at all. The fear is so great that it freezes us into inaction. But this isn't living: it is existing. For others, risk-taking is a way of life, and one crisis follows the other. But the price paid is high; relationships, health and quality of life all suffer. Most of us, however, like to play safe most of the time, with the odd risk here and there, especially if the penalty for losing is not too extreme. But whether we are risk-takers or not, chance will happen to us without being sought out. It is a factor that should always be considered, and it plays a far more active role in our lives than we realise.

Much of life is a gamble. Good and bad luck comes and goes. Lucky people, however, understand something many of us don't: although chance is always a factor, this doesn't mean you have no control. In the words of Niccolo Machiavelli in *The Prince*, 'Fortune is the arbiter of half the things we do, leaving the other half or so to be controlled by ourselves.' Some things in life are out of our hands, but there are also many things that are within our control. And we can take an active part in our lives by turning these things to our advantage.

LUCK THEORIES

In the last few decades scientists have increasingly turned their attention to finding a pattern behind what appears to be random luck. It's exciting stuff. Many things that happen in the world seem to happen randomly, but this is only if you look at them as individual cases. Take all the incidents together and they tend to show a uniform pattern.

For example, throw two dice nine times. See how many times you can get both to show the same number. This may not happen at all, but if you continue to throw the dice over and over again you will eventually see the same numbers come up. Repeat the exercise and it won't be long before the same thing happens again. It's the law of averages.

The same applies to our lives. Should we feel so astonished when good or bad luck strikes? Take road accidents or plane crashes, for example. With all that activity it is inevitable that collisions are going to occur from time to time. It's the law of averages. It's the same with good fortune, like bumping into an old friend or finding that parking spot, and bad fortune, like losing your keys or missing a train. The law of averages dictates that sooner or later both good and bad fortune will find us.

There are also going to be runs of good or bad luck in games of chance or in life itself. We've all heard of a lucky streak or a losing streak, or 'It's my lucky day,' or 'It never rains but it pours.' According to the theory of probability, this can be explained by the fact that when random events occur they tend to cluster now and then. It just happens. This could explain why some people seem to be born lucky. If our destiny is determined by the cosmic roll of a dice, some people will benefit from more luck than others.

What can happen will happen. Roll the dice and a 7 will turn up eventually. Spin the roulette wheel and it will eventually stop on red. Buy a lottery ticket and a certain combination of numbers will eventually win a jackpot. What can happen will happen. This is the gambler's credo: a certain faith that this ticket will win and that this dice will roll. Above all, this is the mantra of mathematicians. They know the limits of certainty and calculate the slender odds on which good or bad fortune rests.

Beat the dealer

In January 1961 a 28-year-old academic named Edward O. Thorp spoke to a meeting of the American Mathematical Society on an unusual topic. His lecture was entitled 'Formula's fortune: a winning strategy for blackjack'.

Two years earlier, while on holiday in Las Vegas, Thorp had become interested in using the mathematical laws of probability to predict the odds on particular cards being dealt as a blackjack game proceeded. Then he took a job as an instructor at the Massachusetts Institute of Technology, where he struggled with the necessary computations, only to conclude that they would take 10,000 years at desk calculators. Not so, said a colleague, who suggested that Thorp try the university's computer. He taught himself how to program the machine, then put it to work. Six months later he had a book-length mass of data. 'The answers amaze me,' Thorp said later. 'The odds fluctuate between dealer and player as successive hands are dealt.'

Thorp used the computer's output to devise an odds-gauging system based on counting face cards and tens (cards most beneficial to players) and also keeping track of fives (cards most beneficial to the dealer). After he described his system to fellow-mathematicians the press got wind of it, and soon he was being offered large sums of money for a trial. He accepted a stake of $10,000 and in thirty hours of play turned it into $21,000—an adventure he subsequently recounted in a book, *Beat the Dealer.*

But the casinos had the last word. Seeing that they could not win against his mathematical logic, they instructed the dealers to shuffle the cards and change packs more frequently, making it difficult for Thorp to keep track of the cards. According to Thorp himself, one dealer went as far as to drug his drink. Eventually, when even those measures failed to defeat Thorp and his card-counting followers, most of the casinos simply declared themselves off limits to the astute mathematicians.

The small world of coincidence has shrunk even more than we think. Yet the dictates of probability ensure that some of life's most desirable events still elude us; depending on the game and which country you live in, the odds of winning a lottery range from one in two million to one in fifty million. Mathematical probability theories aside, there isn't really anything you can do about it, except hope. You either strike lucky or you don't.

Despite efforts to explain logically why things happen when they do, are we any nearer to understanding what Lady Luck is and why it happens? Almost; but there is one drawback. Even though we know that good luck and bad luck will both happen, we have no idea when, where or whom they will strike.

Interesting, but not very helpful to you or me, is it? We don't want to rely on vague guesswork or on hoping against hope any more. What we want to know is: how do we get lucky and stay lucky? That's what the rest of this book is all about.

2

JUST MY LUCK

People who are often unlucky spend most of their time in defence. They let things happen to them without asking why, and all their energy is spent in trying to fight the odds. We all suffer misfortunes. We've just seen that the law of averages dictates that sometimes it is our turn and there isn't much we can do. But while this may be true in some cases, in the majority it isn't. Most of the time what we call bad luck is the result of our failing to take charge of our lives. What we call bad luck becomes a convenient excuse for all sorts of mess-ups.

Often we are the ones at fault, but we haven't the common sense to realise it. When we detect a pattern of bad luck in our lives we should ask ourselves how much we are contributing to these circumstances. We need to understand our role in bringing about unlucky situations and stop blaming luck or other people. How many times a day do you hear people, yourself included, complaining that it is just their luck? It's as if we have absolutely no control over what happens.

> 'I have such lousy luck,' says Jackie. 'Everybody else makes private calls from work, but I was the one who got caught.'

> 'How unlucky can you get!' says Sam. 'I was only five minutes late, and there it was: a great fat parking ticket. It's my third one this year.'

If you are driving at 55 miles/hour in a 50 miles/hour speed limit zone, is it bad luck that you get a fine for careless driving? If you oversleep and are late for an important job interview, is that bad luck or lack of preparation?

Maybe it is time for Sam and Jackie to take a look at how much their own behaviour is contributing to their so-called bad luck and how they are setting themselves up for it. Perhaps it is time to ask themselves whether they are unlucky or causing the circumstances.

Some people have all the luck

Some people have all the luck, you hear people say. But it could be that most people make their own luck. Benjamin Disraeli said, 'We make our destinies and call them fate.' For some, luck is actually the result of careful planning and the ability to take advantage of what comes along.

> Many people thought Judith Keppel was lucky when she became the first person to win a million pounds on the ITV programme 'Who Wants to Be a Millionaire?'. Was it luck? Yes, Judith would be the first to tell you that it was lucky to be asked questions she felt comfortable with. But few people know what Judith did behind the scenes to get on the show in the first place and how clever her strategies were.
>
> Judith influenced the odds of getting on the show by phoning her entry over a thousand times. She then influenced the odds of answering correctly by studying the show and working extremely hard to improve her general knowledge in all subject areas. When she was picked to be a contestant she stayed focused by clearing her head of negative thoughts. And when she was asked questions she wasn't sure of, she was willing to take calculated risks and put herself on the line.

We all know lucky people who seem to dance through life.

Opportunities come their way, and bad things don't slow them down. We love lucky people, but we envy them too. Instead of envying them, we should study them and find out what they do to attract luck.

Talk to people you admire about their achievements. Find out how they got their breaks. Find out how they were given opportunities. Find out how they improved their odds. Find out how they turned disappointment into triumph. That's exactly what I've tried to do for you in this book. I talked to, watched and studied successful people from all walks of life and found out what they did to get lucky and make their own opportunities.

Make your own luck

> One man who made his own good fortune was the architect Ranulf Flambard. He built the Tower of London and then was unlucky enough to be the first man imprisoned in the stout fortress. But he escaped, because, as the architect, he knew a secret way out.

Get lucky

One thing that becomes abundantly clear when you study lucky people is that they have an upbeat outlook, which helps them work a bit harder and a bit smarter to get what they want. They also have the kind of lucky personality that encourages other people to offer them opportunities.

To improve the odds of good things happening to you, the first and last thing you need to do is stop thinking that you don't deserve luck or that luck is a mysterious, unpredictable force you have no control over. If you want to improve your luck, you need to start thinking and feeling lucky.

So before we explore luck-making techniques, let's find out how lucky you think you are.

3

How Lucky Are You?

You can take some of the chance element out of luck by taking a more active role in making good things happen to you. Take some time to think about the following:

Think of someone you know who is luckier than you.

- Why is that person lucky?
- Do you think that person deserves his or her luck?
- What do you think that person does to deserve his or her luck?

For what are you grateful?

- Would you be unhappy without these things or relationships?
- If yes, then do they make you feel happy now to have them?

Think about three good things that have happened in your life.

- What role did you play in influencing these situations?
- What aspects of luck were out of control, and what were in your control?

What are the three unluckiest things that have happened to you?

- What role did you play in your misfortune?
- Would you think and behave differently if you had the chance to go back in time?

If you think about these questions carefully, you may begin to see that you are not always the random guest of misfortune.

Sometimes you play a part in attracting good or bad luck. Hopefully, you'll also start to think that maybe, just maybe, you are luckier than you think.

YOU ARE LUCKIER THAN YOU THINK

> Researchers at the University of Hertfordshire invited fifty people who thought of themselves as lucky and fifty people who thought of themselves as unlucky to take part in a computerised coin-tossing test. Each person was asked to choose head or tails when an elf flipped a coin on a computer screen. When the results were scanned, something interesting occurred. The people who thought themselves lucky had guessed right about the same number of times as those who said they were unlucky. So those who thought they were lucky weren't any more lucky than those who thought they were not.
>
> After conducting these experiments, the psychologists discovered that people who said they were lucky were more likely to remember positive things that happened in their lives and forget the bad. Those who thought they were unlucky remembered mostly the bad things and forgot the good. The study concluded that the reason people think of themselves as lucky is their positive outlook, which helps them work towards their goals. Those who remember mostly the bad things are more likely to mess up or give up.

What this means, for those of us who consider ourselves unlucky, is that we are all a lot luckier than we think we are. All we need to do is start focusing more on the good than on the bad.

And if this isn't enough to convince you, consider the incredible lottery that you won at the moment of conception. At that instant a single cell produced by your mother was travelling through her body. Your father, on the other hand, had millions of sperm cells, all of them different. Something or other—fate, chance, luck, god—chose only one of those sperm to fertilise your mother's egg, thus creating the unique being that is you. Had the egg joined with a different sperm cell, the you that is you would never have existed.

WHAT'S YOUR POINT OF VIEW?

People who think they are unlucky are unlikely to engage in opportunities and more likely to give up. Why bother, they ask themselves. If you think of yourself as unlucky, you are unlikely to be lucky. So the very first thing you need to work on, if you want to improve your chances of luck, is changing your point of view.

Here are some opinions expressed by experts in their fields over the years. At the time they were said they were genuine opinions, and they could have led the recipients to become discouraged. Instead of adopting a pessimistic point of view, however, each of the people below refused to give up. They went on to become lucky in a big way.

> John Grishams's first novel, *A Time to Kill*, was rejected by sixteen agents and a dozen publishing houses. Wynwood Press eventually published 5,000 copies in 1989, but sales were dismal.
>
> (John Grisham became the best-selling author of *The Firm* and *The Pelican Brief*, prompting Dell to publish *A Time to Kill* in paperback in 1992. Sales were huge, and it was made into a film in 1996.)

> At the end of lunch the publisher shook the hand of his latest author and told her, 'You'll never make any money out of children's books, Jo.' The remark has become one of Joanne's favourite stories.
>
> (Joanne's fourth royalty cheque in 1999 after the publication of *Harry Potter and the Philosopher's Stone* had six zeros on it. She was officially a millionaire at the end of June 1999.)

> Elvis Presley's music teacher at Humes High School in Memphis, Tennessee, gave him a C and told him he couldn't sing.
>
> (Elvis became the king of rock and roll, selling more than 600 million albums and singles before his death in 1977.)
>
> Marilyn Monroe was dropped in 1947 by Twentieth Century Fox after one year under contract because the production chief, Darryl Zanuck, thought she was unattractive.
>
> (Marilyn became a Hollywood sex goddess who is still a legend today.)

Just as ridiculous as the opinions offered by the 'experts' above are those made by real people like you and me:

> 'I'm never going to be any good at anything.'
> 'What's the point? I'm going to fail anyway.'
> 'Nobody likes me. There must be something wrong with me.'
> 'Good things never happen to me.'
> 'I'll always be fat.'
> 'I'm always unlucky.'

What do these statements have in common? Firstly, they are all opinions, perceptions about the way things are. Secondly, they are all inaccurate and incomplete, even though the people who said them are convinced they are true.

An opinion is the way you see something, your belief, your frame of reference. It is not a fact: it is just an opinion about what you, or someone else, knows at the time. And that opinion is often inaccurate. Even if you are convinced you are right, things can always change for the better.

Do you think that nothing is ever going to go right for you?

Remind yourself that Ptolemy was just as convinced that the earth was the centre of the universe.

If expecting luck is one of the most vital tools in your luck tool-box, negative expectation is one of the quickest ways to attract bad luck. If you feel good about yourself, not only are you more likely to attract good luck, because you are open to it, but other people are more likely to want to be around you and offer you opportunities. But if you feel bad about yourself, the opposite is true. Opportunities pass you by, because you are too wrapped up in negative expectation to see them; and because other people feel uncomfortable around you, they are unlikely to offer you opportunities that can improve your luck.

In short, to attract luck you need to think and feel lucky.

4

Get a Lucky Attitude

Our brains are photocopiers, cameras, videotape recorders, wide-screen projectors, a thousand computers plus ten million miniature microfilm cartridges, all designed into one storage battery floating in an electromechanical solution. With this virtually untapped and limitless resource, why aren't we more creative, inventive, and successful?

> Laziness is one mental block. Why bother?
> Fear is another big block. It's too much of a risk for me.

But, as we saw in the previous chapter, a low self-image, resulting from negative attitudes about ourselves, is the biggest block preventing us from exploring our full potential.

You are either the captive or the captain of your thoughts. You can resign yourself to failure and mediocrity, or you can dare to dream. Is it foolish to dream of being the first woman prime minister? Margaret Thatcher didn't think so. Foolish to imagine standing on the moon? Neil Armstrong dared to imagine.

> 'The fact is that we literally become what we think about most of the time. Each of us becomes that make believe self we have imagined. But the wonderful thing is we can choose our attitudes. The most important thing to remember right now is that it makes little difference what is actually happening, it's how you personally take it that really counts.' (Earl Nightingale)

Attitude is the answer. In order to be the lucky person you deserve to be, you need to get your head together with constructive self-talk. You need to start thinking and behaving lucky. By changing your thoughts you can change the quality of your life, you can create good or bad luck. What you see in your mind's eye is what you get. Let's remind ourselves again how this works:

> Imagine you woke up feeling low. 'Oh, no, this is going to be a bad day,' you think. You start the day expecting the worst, and that's what you get. You feel grumpy and you look grumpy. Who wants to offer you opportunities in that mood? And if any luck does come along, you will miss it, because you aren't expecting it, or no-one can be bothered to tell you about it.
>
> Start the day again. You wake up feeling low, but you know you can change your attitude. 'Okay, I'm not feeling my best, but I'm going to make this a good day.' And it will be. You smile and try to lift your mood, and those around respond to you. You are high in expectation, so when that great opportunity presents itself you recognise it.

A negative attitude attracts negative people and events into your life. Expect the worst, and you will get the worst. 'You see, I knew it was going to be a horrible day, and it was.' Positive attracts positive. Expect the best and it will happen. Tomorrow when you wake up say, 'I will make this a lucky day.' Give it a try. Expect the best all day, and see what happens.

BORN LUCKY?

In the last few years there have been great advances in the field of genetic research. It is now thought that a number of our personality characteristics have their roots in our unique genetic coding. You are more likely to experience bad luck, for example, if you have been programmed with a temperament that is inclined to become depressed or anxious when under stress. Your auto-response to problems means you have less chance of seeing the positive point of view than someone who is naturally calm in a crisis.

Before you sit back with a sigh and say, 'I told you so: there is nothing I can do about it,' let me draw your attention to even more recent research in the field of neuroscience, which shows conclusively that our brain's habitual thinking patterns continue to be formed and set long after we are born, possibly throughout our lives.

The most formative time is, of course, childhood. This is why the way we were brought up and educated and the way we think about ourselves can have such a powerful effect on our attitudes for the rest of our lives. Negative or positive comments made when you were a child can make all the difference. If your parents or carers were upbeat and positive, you are far more likely to think and feel lucky. If your parents were critical and negative, the chances are you will also lack belief in yourself.

Most of the negative beliefs we have about ourselves have no foundation in reality. We are not lazy, clumsy, stupid, no good, unlucky (I am sure you can add your own personal favourites here). Many of us learned our lessons from an early age when we literally believed what we heard. If, for example, you were told you were stupid as a child or that lucky things didn't happen to your family, you may still hold that belief now. You may be clever and have good things in your life, but deep down you believe otherwise. This belief can affect your whole life and the lives of your children. Children are born copycats. They learn by copying what they see. So in that respect it could be said that good or bad luck runs in families.

If you are negatively inclined or were criticised a lot as a child, this doesn't mean you can't change. *You are only born unlucky if you allow yourself to be.* Just because you have a tendency to feel negative about yourself doesn't mean you have to, or your children have to. You have the power to change your thinking patterns and the way you feel about yourself right now. You can teach yourself to be positive and to expect good things to happen to you.

> Caution: There may be some very legitimate reasons for the pessimistic vision you have of yourself and the world. If you were criticised or abused as a child, suffer from an addiction, or experienced great personal trauma, it's hardly surprising that you have pinned negative labels on yourself. Hopefully this book will help you turn things around so that the world will seem a lot brighter to you. But if your negativity is very deeply ingrained, you may find that you need a therapist to help you overcome negative attitudes and programming. Your first port of call would be your doctor, who can refer you to a counsellor, therapist, or specialist.

Limiting beliefs that block luck

We have seen how damaging negative self-belief can be for your luck. It is equally damaging to have preconceived notions about luck.

One of these limiting beliefs is that luck is just another word for hard work. Yes, you do have to work hard to make luck happen, but hard work does not entitle you to success. Lucky people work smart. They do what is needed to get what they want, but they don't bury themselves in work. It's often the case that working too hard stops you spotting opportunities and taking advantage of them. The way to make luck happen is to expose yourself to as much opportunity as possible, and you can't do that if you haven't got the time or the energy to do it.

The world's most famous pop icon, Madonna, is a good example of someone who took steps to improve the odds in her favour. No-one could describe her as a great singer or dancer. Yet she became a superstar. Why? Because right from the start she behaved like one. Her focus, energy, determination, self-belief, willingness to take risks and sense of humour made her popular.

Madonna is one of those people who is brilliant at looking lucky, being in the right place at the right time, and taking advantage of the many opportunities that are typically made available to people who appear lucky.

Another limiting belief about luck is the idea that it is all about meeting the right people. Yes, you do need to have the right connections to make luck happen in your life, but if you can't create a positive impression when you meet these people, there is little point in meeting them in the first place.

A friend of mine who is a literary agent often comes across people who want to get into print. I remember him telling me about a woman he met at a party who had been trying to find a publisher for her novel for fifteen years. Instead of asking how the publishing process worked, so that she stood a better chance of being published, she spent the entire time talking about herself and how she deserved to be published. Her self-focused approach alienated the agent, and she missed out on an opportunity to learn something that could have helped her get where she wanted to go.

Then there is the belief that lucky people are aggressive self-promoters. This is clearly untrue. The more you brag and talk about yourself, the less likely you are to be offered opportunities. People have to like you to help you get what you want, and nobody likes an egomaniac. Lucky people gently promote themselves and let other people come to their own conclusions. They go for the soft sell, not the hard sell, giving just enough information so that people are left with a positive impression.

'If anyone comes across as too smug, I'm immediately wary,' says Mark, a head-hunter. 'I like to help people who are positive about themselves but not in an obnoxious way. There is nothing guaranteed to create tension in the work-place more than a know-it-all who won't listen to other people's advice or opinions.'

And, finally, there is the belief that luck is just good timing. Luck does require good timing, but being at the right place at the right time is more often in your control than not. Lucky people don't wait for coincidence to smile on them. They take steps to be where opportunity can meet them.

> Barnett Helzberg Junior was walking down a New York street one day when he heard someone say, 'Mr Buffett'. Mr Buffett was one of the wealthiest men in America, and Helzberg knew all about him and the financial criteria he used when considering buying a company. Helzberg was thinking of retiring and selling his company, and he couldn't think of a better buyer than Buffett. So he seized the moment and introduced himself. In May 1995 Buffett bought Helzberg Diamond shops, a chain of stores, for around $300 million.

Helzberg's timely response to a pure chance situation resulted in a turning-point in his fortune. The deal would not have happened if Helzberg hadn't been walking down the same street as Buffett and someone hadn't called out Buffett's name. A few seconds may have made all the difference. Coincidences like this happen all the time and are beyond our control. But when Halzberg recognised who Buffett was, the situation changed. Now he was in control.

If Helzberg had simply walked on, either because he didn't realise the potential of this event or because he chose not to respond, good luck would never have entered the picture. But having recognised the possibilities of this random encounter, he chose to respond to it, thereby transforming his luck to such an extent that it changed his life. He had become to a degree the creator of his life.

Make luck

In this chapter we have seen that lucky people play a key role in influencing their luck. They feel that they deserve good luck, and they live in expectation of it. They don't allow inaccurate points of view to distort their vision about themselves or about luck, and they create luck from chance.

The first step on the road to a luckier and happier life is changing the way you think about yourself and the way you think about luck. All change starts with you.

5

All Change Starts with You

If you want to make a change in your life, the place to begin is not with your partner, your job, your family, your friends, your employers, your wardrobe or your weight but with the way you think and feel about yourself. Everything starts with you. If you don't feel good about yourself to start with, how can you expect other people to feel good about you and offer you opportunities that can improve your luck?

Building self-confidence is a lifelong goal. Don't expect it to happen overnight. Changing from the inside out is one of the main themes of this book. It is also one of the main themes of your life. Everyone has their doubts and fears, no matter how confident they appear. There will always be private battles to fight, and there is nothing wrong with that. The important thing is that you learn how to manage them.

Before diving into luck-making techniques, let's look at how you can immediately start to build your self-confidence and feel good on the inside.

Be kind to yourself

Being kind to yourself can mean many things. It means not expecting yourself to be perfect. It means being patient when you make mistakes and giving yourself time to learn and grow, however old you are. It means taking yourself a little less seriously. It also means forgiving yourself when you make a mistake. Learn from your mistakes, and then put them firmly in the past. Don't keep punishing yourself with them. Learn what went wrong and move on. Make amends if you have to, and look to the future.

It is vital that you take time to care for yourself, to renew and to relax. If you don't, you may lose your zest for life. Take care of yourself by eating healthily, getting enough sleep, exercising, and keeping a sense of balance in your life. Find a place where you can be alone from time to time to get away from the bustle, have a good cry, or simply relax. There are other ways you can renew yourself. Exercise is great, such as going for a run, or a walk, dancing, or playing sports. Watching videos, playing a musical instrument, painting, reading, talking to friends or writing in a journal are just some ways to help you cope.

THE IMPORTANCE OF BEING EARNEST

Lucky people don't build their lives on friends, partners, family or other things, such as work, money, or appearance. Instead, they base their lives on their most deeply held values or principles.

Centring your life around anything else but positive values is a recipe for disaster. If all you think about is work, then an upset at work is going to send you into melt-down. If all you think about is your family, then your life won't be as fulfilling as it should be. If the opinions of your friends are all that matter to you, you will feel vulnerable when those friends move on or let you down. But if you base your life on your values, you will have the inner strength and resolve you need.

What are values? Values are things like honesty, respect, love, loyalty, and responsibility. There are many more, and your heart will easily recognise them. To grasp why positive values are important, imagine your life based on their opposites. It's impossible to be lucky through deception, hate, or anger. Once fooled, people won't trust you or feel comfortable around you, which will not enhance your good fortune. Nobody wants to help a liar or a cheat. In short, living in accord with your values is the only policy if you want to improve your luck.

LUCK-BUSTER: DISHONESTY

> Never trade your morals for your goals. It will bring you enemies and bad luck. If you compromise what you believe in to achieve your goals, you will end up feeling unhappy and make enemies. If you do not believe yourself to be moral, luck will slip through your fingers. People who feel they don't have any morals are rarely as lucky or as happy as those who feel they are moral.[1]

Be honest with yourself, your actions, and the people you meet. There is nothing guaranteed to ruin your chance of luck more than trying to be something you are not. It is impossible to do wrong and feel right. Your conscience won't let you. If other people around you are being dishonest, it takes courage to do what you think is right. But remember, honesty is always the best policy, even if it isn't the popular thing to do.

The nine secrets of lucky people outlined in part 2 are all based on the laws of love and integrity. That's where they get their power from.

CHALLENGE NEGATIVE SELF-BELIEF

If you keep thinking you are unlucky and nothing good can happen to you, sooner or later you will start believing it. Would you trust or believe in someone who kept telling you they were a failure? When you bring yourself down, your self-esteem falls lower and lower. Try not to say bad things about yourself. Instead of 'I can't' say 'I'll do the best I can.' Instead of 'I'm no good at' say 'I'm getting better at.' Instead of 'I always mess up' say 'I always learn from my mistakes.' When you start to put a positive spin on things, your self-esteem improves and others treat you with more respect, which in turn increases your self-esteem and your chances of luck.

Be your own best friend

Do you sometimes hate yourself? Do you criticise yourself when you make mistakes or can't make decisions? This kind of self-hate just makes you feel low, and when you feel low you won't attract luck. Try this exercise to lift you out of negativity.

Imagine that you have stepped outside yourself and are standing by yourself. Become your own best friend. What would you say that would be reassuring and comforting? How would you encourage yourself to become more confident? What would you say to your friend? Would you give him a hug? Would you tell him that he is doing okay and you appreciate how hard things are but you think he is terrific and coping really well?

This exercise is easy and really helpful. When you feel low, become your own best friend and see how much better you immediately feel about yourself.

When you think about yourself, what kind of person do you see? This is hard to do, especially when you are feeling low. Many of us are very critical of ourselves, but most of our negative beliefs have no foundation in reality. Until you can change negative beliefs about yourself you will always doubt your abilities. You change your negative beliefs by training your mind to believe positive things instead. Rather than saying, 'I am stupid,' tell yourself that even though you sometimes do stupid things this does not make you a stupid person. Start to appreciate things about yourself, however small they may be. Appreciate your eyebrows, the way you smile, the way you talk. Begin to admire something about yourself and you will soon learn to appreciate other things about yourself. As you start to appreciate yourself, your self-image will improve, and so will your luck.

Balance yourself

When self-esteem is good, our mind, body, emotions and spirit are balanced. For example, if you spend countless hours in the gym you may neglect your mind. If you spend the whole day thinking and working, by bedtime you will end up feeling uncomfortable. Good self-esteem depends upon a balance of mental, physical, emotional and spiritual activity. If you aren't feeling at your best ask yourself:

> Have I taken care of myself physically today?
> How much mental activity have I had today?
> Have I been in touch with my feelings today?
> Have I had some spiritual time today?

Discover where the imbalance lies, and then find ways to re-create balance in your life. The balance-yourself suggestion box below has some helpful tips that you might want to refer to from time to time. They are all about keeping you feeling good so that you can deal better with life and improve your luck. It means regularly renewing and strengthening the four key areas in your life: your body, your brain, your heart, and your soul.

Balance is absolutely crucial if you want to deal more effectively with life. The best way to explain why is to use imagery. If you are not doing the best for yourself, luck-making can be compared to trying to cut down a tree with a blunt hatchet. It will take you hours. But if you take fifteen minutes to sharpen your hatchet, progress will be much quicker.

Balance-yourself suggestion box

You are what you eat

If you put the wrong kind of petrol in your car it won't run smoothly. The same applies to us. If we eat things that are unsuitable for us we will not feel our best, look our best, or perform our best.

Decide to eat well. Take charge of your food intake and be aware of what you are putting into your body. Make sure you eat lots of vegetables and fruit and an adequate amount of protein. Eat high-fibre carbohydrates and avoid sugar, alcohol, caffeine, and excessive fats. Drink lots of water to clear out toxins. Eating healthily is a great way to boost your self-esteem. If you have been eating things without thought, then try breaking the habit for just one day, first to demonstrate that you do have the strength to control yourself and take in the best nutrients for your body. Then try for two days and so on until eating well becomes a habit that increases your feeling of general well-being.

If you don't have the so-called ideal physique, so what! The important thing is to feel good physically. If you feel good you will look good. In the words of Oprah Winfrey, one of the world's most successful women, who continues to battle with her body image, 'You have to change your perception. It is not about looking right—it is about caring for yourself on a daily basis.'

Exercise

One of the quickest and easiest ways to feel good about yourself is to take regular exercise. So why do so many of us avoid it?

We often make unrealistic promises in the keep-fit department and then we feel bad about ourselves when we can't live up to them. So keep your goals realistic. I'm not suggesting daily visits to the gym or a marathon run. Begin with three ten-minute sessions each week. If you are not used to exercise, have small goals, such as walking short distances instead of driving, or taking the stairs instead of the lift. Small achievements will develop your inclination and motivation to increase your exercise, and once you start to feel better and enjoy the benefits there will be no stopping you.

Sleep

Lack of quality sleep is one of the biggest causes of low self-esteem. Don't panic if you aren't getting eight hours of sleep at night. Everyone has different sleep needs. The best indicator of sleep need is how you feel during the day. Are you alert, energetic, and able to concentrate? If you feel exhausted, irritable and about to doze all the time, you are not getting enough sleep. Here are a few suggestions to help you sleep better. Try to establish regular waking and sleeping times, so that you establish a sleeping pattern. Make sure your bedroom is comfortable and quiet. Avoid heavy meals, exercise and caffeine at least two hours before you go to sleep. Relax as much as you can before you go to bed. Take a warm bath or listen to some soothing music.

Develop an interest

Finding and developing a hobby or talent or special interest is one of the most important things you can do to build your self-esteem. There are all kinds of things you may be good at. You may have a talent for reading, writing, or speaking. You may have a gift for creativity, a good memory, or a talent for helping others. You may have organisational, music or leadership skills. It doesn't matter where your interests lie. When you do something you like, it is a form of self-expression. It's fun, it sharpens your mind, and it builds your self-esteem.

Look for something new

Education doesn't stop when you leave school. Keep learning and discovering all the time. Looking for something new encourages your imagination and interest. Children have a natural interest in the world around them. Unfortunately, as we get older we lose this interest in life, and this can lead to fatigue and boredom. Re-awaken your interest in life by doing something new. An adventurous spirit encourages creativity, excitement, and good feelings about yourself. Do something different. Go to a concert to listen to some music you don't normally listen to, sign up for an evening class, learn a new language, visit a place where you have never been, vary your routine. The possibilities are endless. When you do something new you always feel more energetic and learn something new about yourself.

TAKE CARE OF YOUR HEART

Our feelings are very important, but we often don't know what we are feeling. If you aren't in touch with your feelings you can't be true to yourself, and self-esteem will be low. Give yourself feeling checks throughout the day. Stop and ask yourself, 'What am I feeling?' 'Why does this make me feel a certain way?' 'Does this feel good?' 'Does this feel bad?' This will help you become more aware of your feelings and help you recognise your needs.

And when everything seems to be going pear-shaped or you do something really stupid, keep your heart healthy and strong by laughing.

> 'Laughter, *n.* An interior convulsion producing a distortion of the features and accompanied by inarticulate noises. It is infectious and, though intermittent, incurable.' (Ambrose Bierce)

Sometimes life stinks and there is nothing you can do about it, so you may as well laugh. Learn to laugh at yourself when strange or stupid things happen to you, because they will.

TAKE CARE OF YOUR SOUL

When we forget to pay attention to our spirits, we become nervous, stressed, and afraid. We are all creatures of the earth, and the world will offer us support and calm if we take the time to connect with it.

One of the most effective ways to calm your mind is to get in touch with nature. Plan to escape the town or city even if only for a few hours a week. If this isn't possible, take a walk in the park. Take time to appreciate the wonders of nature, the colour of the sky, the green of the grass, the song of the birds. Slow down for a while and enjoy the peace and quiet. It is surprising how quickly you can restore yourself in this way. Low self-esteem is often the result of trying too hard to keep up with the pressures of modern life and neglecting our souls. Take a natural break, enjoy the simple pleasures, and restore your self-esteem.

Another way to relax and feel calm is to physically ground yourself. Become aware of your breathing, and slow it down till you feel calmer. Close your eyes and breathe deeply from your stomach. When you are ready, open your eyes and bring yourself slowly back into the room.

To lead a balanced life with inner strength and self-esteem we need to be able to stop doing and sometimes just be. Just being releases tension and increases our self-awareness. Spend a few minutes each day in total silence. Turn off the television or radio. Don't read a book or do anything. This will be difficult at first, so don't sit for too long. As you get used to it, you will be able to do it for longer and be able to balance your being with your doing.

Stop hoping and start doing

Now that you are working on your self-esteem, it is time to start creating the kind of life you want. In the past if you wanted something there seemed to be only two ways: working hard or hoping for a stroke of random good luck. Unfortunately, neither strategy guarantees success. We all know people who work eighty hours a week and never achieve their dreams. When hard work disappoints, many people give up striving and start wishing. The stock market, the lottery, the casino, all hold out the promise of getting something without having to work hard. We get excited when we hear of instant success and we want it for ourselves. The problem with hoping for good fortune is that, as we have seen, the odds are stacked against us—about a million to one, to be precise. So if you are waiting for good luck to change your life, you may have to wait for a long, long time.

But now you are learning that there is another way to get what you want in life. You can create your own luck. Lucky people are like the rest of us: they work hard and wish for good things, but what makes them special is what they do to make good luck happen to them.

So let's stop hoping and start doing. In the chapters that follow you'll find out what you can do to create luck in your life. You will find out how you can make your attitudes and actions so compelling that nearly everyone you meet will want to offer you opportunities. And so, if you are ready, let's go and create some luck together.

PART TWO

Nine Secrets of Lucky People

The root of the word *happiness* is *hap*—an ancient word that means luck or chance. You can see this meaning in words like *haphazard* (aimless or determined by chance) or even *happen*, when something occurs by chance without planning. A long time ago a person's luck, good or bad, used to be referred to as one's *hap*. The link between happiness and good luck is built in to the English language.

Mastering the skills outlined in this book may not guarantee that you will have it all—win the lottery or find the man or woman or whatever of your dreams; but you will find yourself feeling a whole lot happier. And at the end of the day, aren't luck and happiness the same thing? Think about it: if you aren't happy, are you really lucky?

6

Lucky Secrets

Developing a good-luck personality isn't difficult. Most of the skills lucky people possess can be mastered by anyone. If you want to be lucky, all you need to do is start behaving lucky.

Scientists and psychologists devote careers to finding out what makes people feel and behave lucky. Their research is all too often hidden in obscure journals and reports, inaccessible to the lay person. In this section you'll discover seventy of the most compelling and important studies on luck and happiness in recent years, simplified and summarised into the nine qualities that govern the lives of happy people. Incorporating these qualities into your life will significantly improve your chances of luck.

By now you are probably wondering what these qualities are, so let's end the suspense. Here they are, followed by a brief explanation:

1. Get curious.
   Be willing to experiment and to explore new possibilities.
2. Find out what you want.
   Define your mission and goals in life.
3. Get time on your side.
   Have patience in the right dose. Learn to manage your time well.
4. Look and sound lucky.
   Be the kind of person other people want to help.
5. Don't have enemies.
   Consider everyone a potential lifeline.

6. Balance giving and receiving.
   Be generous with your time and resources and receive help with gratitude.
7. Use your intuition.
   Trust yourself to make the right decisions.
8. Turn rejection into resolve.
   Respond to life with resilience.
9. Push your luck.
   Don't just look and sound lucky; feel lucky too.

The nine qualities mentioned above build upon each other. The first three are associated with self-awareness and self-mastery. Numbers 4, 5 and 6 will help get other people on your side so that you are more likely to be offered lucky opportunities. The final three relate to and inspire the other qualities.

The qualities appear simple, but they can be incredibly powerful. One way to understand them better is to look at their opposites:

1. Be inflexible.
   Expect everything to go the way you want all the time, and if it doesn't, get really angry.
2. Don't have goals.
   Avoid goals at all costs. Live for the moment and forget about tomorrow.
3. Be impatient.
   Try to ensure that everything you want happens right now, irrespective of the needs of others.
4. Brag about your achievements.
   Make sure everyone knows how wonderful you are. Always be the one talking and giving opinions, and don't waste time listening. Why should you try to get along with other people? You have the best ideas, so it's up to them to make the effort for you.

5. Take, take, take.
   Survival of the fittest. You need all the help you can get.
6. Never compromise.
   Don't apologise, say thank you, or sort out disagreements.
7. Ignore your hunches.
   Even if you are not sure you are doing the right thing, go ahead and do it anyway.
8. Give up easily.
   If things don't work out the first time, give up and feel sorry for yourself.
9. Expect bad luck.
   Always concentrate on the negatives and ignore the positives.

As you can see, these attitude problems are recipes for disaster. Yet many of us indulge in them. Is it any wonder life doesn't always work out as planned?

MAKE LUCK A HABIT

Habits are things you do repeatedly. They become part of your life. Many times you aren't even aware that you have them. Some habits, like being polite, exercising regularly, and eating healthy food, are good. Others, like negative thinking and interrupting others when they speak, are bad; and some, like playing with your hair, tapping your fingers, or walking on the cracks in pavements, don't matter that much.

Habits are powerful factors in our lives. They express our character and therefore can make or break us. Fortunately, habits can be broken. They can be learned and unlearned, and you can change your habits any time you like. For example, if you have ever driven on the other side of the road in a foreign country it feels pretty strange at first. But if you drive on the other side for a month it starts to feel more natural. After six months you don't have to think about it any more, because it's now habitual to drive on the other side.

The only way to get rid of negative habits that are holding you back is to replace them with positive ones. And the good news is that you can change negative habits with positive ones any time you choose. I'm not saying it is easy, but I am saying it is possible.

Don't expect these new habits to feel natural right away. Learning a new skill takes time. If there aren't results after a few days or weeks, don't give up. Experts believe that twelve weeks can be a decisive turning-point for new habits to form and old habits to fade away. It is human instinct to be uncomfortable with change, so give it time and ease yourself into new routines.

Don't try to conceal your difficulties: acknowledge them. Comfort yourself with the thought that you are about to embark on an adventure unlike anything you have ever known. And don't expect every idea in this book to work for you. You don't have to be perfect to see results. Just working on some of the qualities will help you experience lucky breaks you might never have thought possible.

7

Get Curious

Lucky people adapt when things don't go according to plan. This doesn't mean they don't have conviction: it means they are curious, open-minded, willing to experiment and explore new possibilities in their search for a solution.

Keyword: Passion

Lucky people are curious, open-minded people. This means they are willing to consider new ideas and possibilities, however crazy they may seem. Narrow-minded people, on the other hand, miss out on opportunities because they are so attached to their rigid routines that when something out of the ordinary occurs they discount it, refusing to budge from what is safe and familiar.

In research[2] on older Americans, the factor that determined satisfaction more than financial stability and current relationships was a willingness to adapt and change. If they were willing to change their routines, habits and expectations they could remain happy even when outward circumstances changed. Those who were resistant to change, on the other hand, were less likely to feel happy.

Lucky people understand that the world is constantly changing. They are willing to try new things in order to put themselves in luck's path.

Are you a curious, open-minded person? Are you interested in other people's points of view? Are you willing to try new things, consider other ways of doing things?

In your eyes

People who are curious and open-minded can see things from another person's point of view. This is the definition of empathy. Empathy is not sympathy. Sympathy is feeling *for* someone; empathy is feeling *with* them. Empathy is looking at the world through another person's eyes.

Ask yourself some questions:

> How would I like to have a friend like me?
> How would I like to have a partner like me?
> How would I like to have a mother or a father like me?
> How would I like to have a manager or an employee like me?
> How would it feel to be an asylum-seeker?
> How would it feel to be homeless and begging for money?
> How does the world appear through the eyes of a teenager or a young child or elderly person?

Take a look at the world from the point of view of anyone you think of as different from you in some way. Lucky people understand that, however much they know, there are always different viewpoints to consider. 'I hadn't thought of that,' 'I see your point,' 'How about trying it another way?' are the lucky person's mantras.

Be flexible

We often want things to be on our own terms. But lucky people think not only about what they want but also about the other person's point of view. They accept that there will always be differences between people, and they know that if you are flexible life can be more satisfying and enjoyable.

We all experience change in our lives and our values over time. Studies[3] show that those who viewed these changes as inevitable and remained open to change were far more likely to be satisfied with their lives than those who did not. One of the hallmarks of unlucky people is a feeling of 'stuckness', of not being able to change anything for the better and so feeling out of control. In order to feel good about yourself you need to feel you have some control. You can do this by being more flexible.

Start with changing something about your life. Choose something that seems to be very insignificant. Break a minor habit. Don't try anything drastic, such as resigning your job, stopping smoking, or ending a relationship. You need to start with small changes that won't cost much energy but will instigate change in your life. Change your hairstyle, buy some different kinds of food, go to bed a little earlier or later, go to work by a different route, read the paper from back to front, and so on. As you start to do things differently you will start to recognise how much control you have over your habitual behaviour patterns. Self-change, even in small ways, starts a process that can pull you out of your rut, encourage you to be flexible, and put you in the path of new possibilities.

The impossible can happen

Narrow-minded people miss opportunities because when something better presents itself they are so wrapped up in their familiar routines or negative beliefs about themselves or others they can't see it. When you have the flexibility to consider other ways of doing things you can make luck from a vast playing-field rather than a narrow little corner of one room. Who knows what you can learn? The world becomes a place of possibilities rather than restrictions and limitations. Luck often happens when we open our minds to believing that what may seem impossible is really possible, either through chance or through some solution we haven't yet thought of.

Columbus's lucky break

> When Christopher Columbus arrived in the New World in 1492 it was partly due to a lucky drink of water. In the 1480s he had been one of many adventurers who believed that it would be possible to sail west and reach the spice-rich Indies, but he had no luck finding a royal backer to finance the trip. Year after year he travelled to the courts of Europe, but he was repeatedly ignored. In all, Columbus spent eight years trying to raise funds for his great adventure. Eventually he went back to the Spanish court for yet another audience with Ferdinand and Isabella. After listening to him they once again turned him down. It was a very hot day, and so after leaving court Columbus stopped at a nearby monastery to get a drink. He started talking to one of the monks, and before long he was pouring out his heart about the journey he longed to make. The monk, as it happened, was the Queen's confessor. And he was so impressed with Columbus's resolve that he spoke to Isabella, who granted Columbus yet another audience. This time, at long last, the King and Queen said yes.

Sometimes luck is available and we simply don't know it yet. Lucky people are a little like fishermen. They have to be optimistic or they would not go fishing, for they are always expecting luck in a few minutes or tomorrow. They are always hopeful that better luck is just around the corner. If you are open-minded you are better able to search for a solution, even when a solution seems impossible, because you are willing to experiment and try out new actions that will broaden your life. You never know: this may bring you luck in forms that you hadn't thought of or asked for.

Bend but don't break

Luck-makers are willing to reconsider their positions when life gives them a reason to reconsider it. You must have values and beliefs to guide you: these define who you are. It is not good to become a reed blown in the wind, changing your beliefs and ideas every time you are exposed to something new. You do need consistency, but you also need to be open-minded enough to adapt your plans if need be.

> 'If bad luck can wrench control from our grasp, so can good luck. The bold are ready to grab a piece of good luck when it drifts by, even if it means going off in a new, unplanned direction. They don't try to control their lives so rigidly that they ignore lucky breaks lying off the main track.'
>
> (Max Gunther)

Lucky people are self-aware enough to know who they are and what they believe in, but they are also open-minded and constantly adding to their knowledge through experience, insight, feedback, and judgment. That way they don't shut out options that could potentially bring luck.

KEEP YOUR EYES AND YOUR EARS OPEN

You must explore new possibilities if you want to strike lucky. In other words, you must keep your eyes and your ears open. Keep learning, read magazine articles and books, search the internet, meet a wide variety of people, visit new places, follow up leads. You need to do this knowing that many of your efforts will not be rewarded. Lucky people are always hungry for experience, because experience gives them insight and because they know that somewhere in all the information-gathering they will eventually find what they want.

The luck expert Max Gunther compares life to a river in his book *How to Get Lucky*. Lots of things you can plan, such as going to school and going on holiday, but some things are completely chance occurrences, like bumping into an old friend, which can often dramatically change your life for the better. To increase your chances of having a life-changing lucky event you need to go where the flow of events is fastest.

Lots of lucky people consciously or unconsciously go where the action is. They stay informed, in the thick of things, circulate at parties, and keep their ears to the ground.

NETWORKING

One of the buzz-words of the 1980s was *networking*, and it is just as important today. Keep your connections with other people alive and you maximise your chances of luck. It's people who become isolated and out of touch who are least likely to get lucky breaks. Why? Because luck almost always comes through some other person.

Try to talk to all kinds of people. Through them you will get fresh observations and novel ideas. The greater your circle of friends and acquaintances, the better your chances of discovering golden opportunities. How many times have you heard that so-and-so got a job, met the love of their life or did this or that, and all because they knew a friend of a friend?

According to sociologists, the average person is in direct contact with something like 300 other people—ranging from family members to colleagues and people you don't know very well at all, like the receptionists at your dentist. If you think that each of those people you know is also in contact with 300 other people, that means your network includes 90,000 people. Now think that each of those 90,000 people is in contact with 300 other people, and your friend-of-a-friend-of-a-friend network increases to 27 million people.

KEEP READING

People who read books benefit both from what they learn and from the entertainment books give them. Most importantly, they get to use their brain. Reading books—fiction and non-fiction—

fires your imagination and broadens your mind. Research[4] shows that regular readers are more likely to be happy with their lives, because reading exercises the imagination and the memory.

What would you rather be, a person who can't concentrate or a person who has a good attention span? A person who reads third-rate work or a person who has access to the greatest minds? A person who reads the same story over and over again with the same plot and characters or a person with imaginative choices? Talk to lucky people. You'll find that books have a lot to answer for.

Switch the Television Off

Television can be a brilliant source of information, but too much of it can distract us from living. Too often we watch television because that is what we usually do and we can't be bothered to think of anything else. Psychologists have found that watching too much television can actually inhibit a person's ability to carry on a conversation—not very helpful if you want people to create luck and get other people on your side. Television robs us of our time, and it doesn't really give us anything back. Watching your favourite serial when you get home is relaxing, but spending the whole evening watching television is a waste of time.

According to one study,[5] television can make us more materialistic and reduce our happiness by about 5 per cent for every hour a day we watch. Another study[6] suggested that television changes our view of the world and can encourage us to develop unrealistic and damaging conclusions that can reduce our chances of luck and happiness by up to 50 per cent. When we watch too much television it is hard not to come to the conclusion that everyone is rich or glamorous or that something horrible is about to happen. It is crucial to separate what you know from television from what is real.

A report from the Harvard Medical School published in the

British Journal of Psychiatry on 1 June 2002 found a significant link between television and symptoms of eating disorders in teenage girls. Dr Anne Becker conducted her research in Fiji, a nation relatively new to the mass media and noted for traditionally encouraging good appearances and larger body shapes. She found that within three years of being introduced to television almost three-quarters of the study's subjects now felt themselves to be too big or too fat.

When you turn on the television, watch only what you really want to watch. Use your newly discovered free time to do something with your family or friends or to learn a new skill. Try doing something that is actively stimulating instead of passively distracting.

Learn to use a computer

Five years ago I moved from central London to live in Dallas, Texas, for two years. For the first six months I was miserable. I had a hard time adapting to a new way of life. I refused to learn to drive or use a computer.

Eventually I realised that if I was to survive I would have to learn to drive. Texas is such a huge place that you can't exist without a car. And if I was to keep up with my friends and family in Britain, e-mail was the best option. I would have to stop hating computers and learn how to use them. Almost immediately my world opened up. I got involved in the local community and started to make friends. And learning to access the internet helped me launch my writing career. I'm still in e-mail contact with the editor who gave me my first book contract.

In a study[7] of older people introduced to personal computers, life satisfaction significantly improved. Whatever age you are, a computer allows you to experience the wonders of technology and the world. If you know where to look, the internet can be a valuable information warehouse and research tool. It also offers access to e-mail, which can not only bring people together who are constantly moved apart but also be one of the best ways to keep in regular no-pressure-to-respond contact with people who may be able to offer you opportunities.

What have you got to lose?

Stay open to opportunities, even if they're long shots. What have you got to lose?

> One of the many hopefuls who answered the call for a part in the film *Mad Max* was the then unknown Australian actor Mel Gibson. The night before his screen test he was attacked and badly beaten up by three drunks. With a 'What have I got to lose?' attitude, Gibson showed up the next morning looking like a prize fighter on a losing streak. It just so happened that the director, George Miller, was looking for someone to play the lead who looked weary, beaten up, and scarred. He gave Gibson the part. It launched Gibson's career as an international star in such films as *The Year of Living Dangerously*, *Lethal Weapon*, and the Oscar-winning *Braveheart*.

There is a strong connection between keeping an open mind and creating luck. 'Why not? What have I got to lose?' is a luck-making attitude. Sometimes your actions will be rewarded and sometimes they won't, but you put yourself in luck's path more often by suspending your logical mind and trying something that seems unconventional, risky, or downright silly. Often just asking yourself, 'Why not? What have I got to lose?' allows you to make progress. Perhaps the job, the partner, the house or the holiday of your dreams is just around the corner.

A LEAP INTO THE UNKNOWN

Sometimes to improve your luck you simply have to take a leap into the unknown. Many people fear challenges, because they see them as obstacles. Lucky people, on the other hand, embrace challenge. They are willing to take risks that might improve their situation, because they know that even if things don't work out they will have gained from the experience.

Fear of failure is the biggest reason many people don't want to embrace a challenge. So how do you teach yourself not to be afraid of challenges? One way is to think about how to address your biggest fears. Let's say, for example, you have been offered a job with added responsibilities. The positive side is better money, new contacts, and new opportunities; the negative side is that the new job may be too demanding for you and you may see less of your friends and family. There is also the danger that you might not enjoy it or even be good at it, and you will have left the security of your present job behind.

In this case the biggest fear seems to be the fear of not being up to the job. To minimise that, a careful assessment of the responsibilities attached to the job and what kind of help and support you get would be necessary. You could also carefully negotiate your hours so that your family and friends don't suffer.

Another strategy to use when embracing challenge is to take it slowly. A friend of mine recently turned down a job as a reporter on a national newspaper because she was afraid of failing and leaving behind the security of her present job in publishing. The trouble was that she imagined the worst and missed out on opportunities and new contacts. The way to embrace challenges comfortably is to do so from a safe place. Perhaps my friend should have taken some freelance work basis the paper first to see if the life-style suited her.

If you fear challenges, think of them as learning experiences. No matter what happens, you will learn from the experience. Doing something different is always scary at first, but once you realise you will become wiser and stronger from the experience, whatever the result, it gets a little easier to take the plunge.

> Mary has learned to think of fear as her intuition telling her to go for it. 'Three years ago I left my comfortable job in the city to freelance from home. The first day I started work on my own I remember feeling absolutely terrified. Was I making the worst mistake of my life? I realised I had to make a choice. I could give it all I had, or I could go back to my old way of life. So I took a deep breath and made that first phone call. I haven't looked back since and now own a successful and profitable home business. Whenever I have fears—I recently hired someone to work with me—I think of how it all started and how successful I have been so far.'

When you face a new challenge, one strategy that works is to make sure you find someone with the experience to help and guide you. When I was given my first book contract I made a mess of it and couldn't meet my deadline. When I finally convinced an editor that I really did have a book in me this time, I got in touch with a bookcrafter to help me create a book that was coherent and well put together. Even today, as I write this, my fourteenth book, I continue to learn on the job. Every book is a new adventure as I explore new areas of human interest.

Think of fear as a bully and confront it. Don't allow yourself to be pushed around. Stand up for yourself. The worst that can happen is that the challenge doesn't work out, but you will have learned from the experience and perhaps even made new friends or contacts who can offer you opportunities in the future. Remember that even great disappointments don't last for ever.

Studies[8] of thousands of Americans show that happy people are not immune to negative events. Instead they have the ability to think about other things in the aftermath of such occurrences. They know that disappointments are important and serious, but the distress will pass and take them in new directions. At any moment they could meet a person or experience a situation that could change their life. And at the very least they can put the disappointment down to life experience and be able to talk about it with insight should the topic of conversation arise with people who may one day be important in their lives. This doesn't mean that you don't feel grief or disappointment when things go badly: it means that you get curious about what life is bringing, instead of what you thought you wanted.

CURIOSITY

When we were children we were blessed with a natural curiosity and awareness. Every day was an exciting adventure filled with wonder and fascination. Our minds were vigorous and active, and we were able to learn things faster and better than we do now.

Sir Isaac Newton, according to the legend, gained his insight into the physical properties of gravity when he sat under an oak tree and an apple hit his head. Similarly, when Archimedes got into an overfull bath, displacing the water over the edge, he shouted 'Eureka!' because at that very moment he knew how to measure the volume of an object by water displacement.

Great minds are often impressed with a heightened sense of awareness. Some of the greatest discoveries of all time would never have been made without curiosity. Edison, Marie Curie, Pasteur and Fleming were all curious people who followed through on seemingly trivial, chance events, turning them into good luck for themselves and all humankind.

We tend to see and hear only what's important to us. For example, if you or your partner is pregnant, suddenly the world seems to be full of pregnant women. In fact the pregnant women have always been there: you just haven't been aware of them. We see and hear only what is important to us and filter out the rest. So sharpen your awareness by continually seeking out new experiences and new information. Develop the habit of looking at things as if it were for the first time. Be alert: lucky breaks are more likely to present themselves.

ENTHUSIASM

What's the quickest way to become old, tired, and cynical? Lose your enthusiasm. In the words of Henry Thoreau, 'None are so old as those who have outlived enthusiasm.'

Remember the first time you went on a bus or a train or an aeroplane? Remember how exhilarating it was? As a child you were filled with breathless wonder. You were utterly fascinated by even the smallest things, like twigs, candles, insects, birds. At that time in your life every day was an exciting adventure. But as you grew up all that began to change. Life became more complicated, with more responsibilities. Gradually you started to shut out interest in things that weren't relevant to your purposes. The light of enthusiasm began to dim.

As our natural enthusiasm fades, so does our capacity to enjoy life. Routine, responsibility and money-making start to take their toll, and it is harder and harder to rid ourselves of the shadow of pessimism.

Wouldn't it be great if you could suddenly have a sparkling new life filled with fun and laughter again? Well, you can. You simply need to recapture the child's heart that you have lost. Enthusiasm can generate enormous energy, sweeping away discouragement and failure and rekindling self-confidence.

The significance of enthusiasm in attracting good luck cannot be overstated. Ralph Waldo Emerson once said, 'Nothing great was ever achieved without enthusiasm.' Enthusiasm creates energy; don't underestimate its power. Medical science has proved that patients who maintain a positive attitude and are enthusiastic about life tend to recover from serious illness faster. Research[9] shows that if you feel enthusiastic about something you are doing, you are more likely to be good at it. Enthusiasm is the excitement you feel inside yourself when you enjoy what you are doing. By unleashing boundless energy you open the door to achievement. You release your own drive and vitality, and you reach your potential by overcoming adversity and achieving goals with energy to spare.

As you begin to rediscover your enthusiasm you will notice an amazing transformation. Your whole outlook will become brighter. You'll discover a zest and a sparkle to your life. Other people will see the change and react differently to you, because they are naturally attracted and inspired by those who are enthusiastic. And your luck will change because luck always favours those who are motivated by enthusiasm.

Be Proactive

The curious, open-minded and enthusiastic nature of lucky people encourages them to be proactive. Every day we have many chances to choose between being proactive and reactive. The weather is bad, you suffer a disappointment at work, you miss the train, you get a parking ticket. So how do you respond? Do you fly off the handle? Do you shout and scream? Or do you make a decision to deal with what comes up and move on? The choice is yours.

Reactive people make choices on impulse. They are like reeds blowing in the wind. If the wind gets strong they break. Proactive people think first and then act. They recognise that they can't always control what happens to them, but they can control the way they react. They are calm and cool and in control. They don't let other people or things upset them or ruin their day.

> Have a think about this:
> Someone you thought was your friend is being negative about you behind your back. She doesn't know you overheard the conversation. You feel hurt and betrayed.

Reactive choices:

- Hit her.
- Get depressed.
- Give her the cold shoulder.
- Spread vicious rumours about her.

Proactive choices:

- Confront her calmly and tell her how you feel.
- Forgive her.
- Give her a second chance. Understand that she has weaknesses just like you and that you too may have talked behind a person's back without meaning any harm.

You can usually tell when you are being reactive by the language you use. 'That's just the way I am' is typical reactive language. What it really means is, 'I have no responsibility for the way I am. I can't change.' When you say, 'If he or she hadn't done that, things would be different,' what you are really saying is that someone else is the cause of your problems. When you say, 'You just made me feel bad,' what you are really saying is 'I am not in control. You are.' When you say, 'If only I had lived somewhere else, been in another job, had more money,' and so on, what you are really saying is 'I am not in control of my happiness, things are. I'm a victim. Everyone has it in for me, and the world owes me something.'

Notice that reactive language takes power away from you and gives it to someone else or something else. It's like saying to someone or something, 'You are in charge of my mood. Do with it what you like.' Proactive language, on the other hand, puts control back with you. You are then free to choose how you behave.

Reactive language:

That's just the way I am. There is nothing I can do. I have to.

Proactive language:

I'll do it. I can do better than that. Let's consider the options. I choose to.

Voltaire likened life to a game of cards. Each player must accept the cards life deals. But once they are in our hands we each must decide how to play the cards in order to win the game. You can't always control what happens to you, but you can control how you respond. You have the power to rise above whatever has been passed down to you.

Take control

Take responsibility for your life and have a can-do attitude. If you are can-do and you are enthusiastic and persistent, it's amazing what you can accomplish. Seize the initiative to achieve your goals. If you are feeling bad about your love life, do something about it. Find ways to meet people. Be friendly and try smiling a lot. Ask other people out. They may not know how great you are. If you need a better job, don't wait for the perfect one to find you. Go after it. Can-do isn't being aggressive and pushy, it is simply being enthusiastic, enterprising, and resourceful.

You don't need to succeed in everything you do to feel happy, but you do need to believe that you have control over your life. Research[10] suggests that those who feel they are responsible for their own decisions are often more satisfied with their lives than those who are not. People are happiest when they allow their individual personality to express itself, not when they try to conform to someone else's identity. We all have the need to belong, and there is nothing wrong with this, as long as you keep a mind of your own and an awareness of your individual identity.

The same applies to social expectations and stereotypes. For example, men who feel they must act tough and women who feel they must be soft are boxed in by expectations that have nothing to do with who they are. It is important to act the way you think is appropriate, not the way you think you are supposed to act. If you are a man and you are at a funeral, there is nothing wrong with tears. If you are a woman and you are quite reserved, you don't have to open up and show your emotions to others. Satisfaction in life has not been found to be connected in any way to how men and women fit into stereotypes of femininity and masculinity.[11] Don't feel you have to conform. Be yourself.

It's your choice

The winning person realises that everything in life is a choice—even being alive. Interviews on life satisfaction[12] found that those who felt they had a choice about what they did or did not do were three times more likely to feel satisfied than those who felt they did not have a choice.

> For example, you may think you have to work, but in fact working is a choice you make because you value the money you receive for it or you love your family and want to take care of them. Every day you go to work you are doing it because you choose to. You choose working over the alternatives: not having enough money to buy food or keep a roof over your head or take care of your children. When you see the options that you have you can begin to appreciate the choices you make. Think of the positive effects of your actions, the reasons you go to work, the reason you keep your household running.

You don't have to do anything. You decide to do things because they are profitable to you and the best choice among the alternatives available to help you along the right path. People who have to do things are usually unlucky because their lives are not in their control. People who choose to do things are usually lucky because their lives are in their control.

Taking control of ourselves means taking the responsibility for making the best use of what we have: our minds, our talents and developed abilities, and that precious little time we have to spend on living. Of course you can't control everything. It is important to appreciate how awesome and mysterious the universe can be and to be humble enough to understand that we can never have complete control. But lucky people operate with a sense of percentages. If you think that we have no control over about 50 per cent of life, that still leaves you with 50 per cent that you can control. So you may as well always start with the attitude that the odds on succeeding are fairly good.

Each one of us has many more choices and alternatives than we are willing to admit. And lucky people aware of these choices get behind the wheel firmly in the driver's seat. They take control of the choices they make, and their lives. They create their own horoscopes. With an open mind they seek opportunity. They dream and they build, but above all they think and act for themselves.

TAKE ACTION TODAY TO ENCOURAGE YOUR CURIOSITY AND OPEN YOUR MIND

1. Be more curious about everything in the world. Read books, listen to audio cassettes, read papers and magazines. Go to seminars and lectures concerning a healthy mind and body. Schedule a check-up with your doctor and ask questions. Seek out and gain counsel from the most interesting and successful people in your profession and hobbies.

2. Break the daily routine you have set. Unplug the television for a week. Go to work by a different route or another mode of transport. Meet new people. Take a holiday to somewhere you would never normally think of going. If you shower, take a bath; if you wear black, wear white. Have you any clothes you

haven't worn for a couple of years? Clear your mind and your wardrobe of old memories and throw out your old clothes, or give them to someone who will wear them.

3. When you walk into a room, instead of feeling self-conscious, concentrate on the people there. Ask them how they are, find out about their lives. Learn as much as you can about them.
4. Take thirty minutes every day for yourself. Relax and breathe deeply. Inhale from the pelvis and stomach right up into your lungs. Exhale slowly. Let go, as if you were lying in the centre of a waterbed the size of a football field. Float freely. Give yourself this half-hour every day to be completely aware that your life belongs to you and that all that exists in your life is seen out of your eyes and experienced by your mind and body.
5. Remember, everything you think is your opinion, based on your impressions from limited resources. Keep expanding your resources from the best authorities. View everything with an open-minded scepticism. Be open-minded enough to explore it without prejudice and sceptical enough to test its validity.
6. Listen to what other people have to say and consider their viewpoint. Consider where they are coming from before criticising and passing judgment. Pay special attention to children and the elderly.
7. When something doesn't work out or you don't get the job or the holiday you dreamed of, don't give up. Try looking for similar jobs or alternative holiday ideas. Think about your wildest dreams. Then assess how much you are hesitating out of fear, and consider what you have to lose if you don't follow your dream. Perhaps the job, the house, the mate or whatever you long for is waiting for you to make the first move.
8. For the next month go all-out in your present job, course,

relationship or whatever you feel is most important to you right now. Dedicate yourself just for four weeks, not a lifetime, to giving the maximum effort to your job, your routine, and your service to other people. At the end of that time you may well find that your enthusiasm has returned.

9. Listen carefully to yourself today. Count how many times you use reactive language, such as 'you make me,' 'I have to,' 'why can't they.' Count to ten before you react to someone who bumps into you, cuts in front of you, or says something you don't agree with.

8

Find Out What You Want

One of the biggest problems for unlucky people is not having a clear idea of what they want in life. Indecision creates inaction, and inaction means you don't get what you want.

Keyword: Focus

Once you start to open your mind and become more aware of the options available to you, the next step is to decide what you want. Rather than waiting for opportunities to come to them, lucky people have goals, and they identify the people who can help them achieve those goals.

Why goals are important

Isn't there something to be said for a lack of ambition and a live-for-the-moment, go-with-the-flow attitude? Clearly, we need to enjoy the moment and not have our heads in the clouds. But going with the flow, without a clear idea of where you want to go, more often than not leads downhill. You end up doing what other people are doing. The road to anywhere is a road to nowhere. Without goals it is all too easy to follow anyone who is willing to take the lead, even into things that won't get you far.

Lucky people rarely follow the herd. They know what they want, whether or not their friends, family, colleagues or partners want it as well.

Too often people choose goals based on what parents, partners, friends, colleagues, employers, the media or other people think. Of course you need to be aware of other people's needs, but it is crucial that you think about what matters to you and set meaningful goals to accomplish what you care about.

It has been said, 'If you don't know where you're going—you're there.' We all know people who appear to drift aimlessly through life, never achieving their dreams. Unfortunately, a person without a goal is no better off than a ship without a rudder. This approach makes your journey through life like that of an unguided missile. 'Great minds have purposes,' said Washington Irving. 'Others have wishes.'

Your brain is a goal-seeking machine. Program it with your goals and it will start to seek out opportunities that can make them happen.

FIND YOUR PURPOSE

Lucky people are convinced and committed about what they want. It is this certainty that gives them the strength and the determination they need to achieve their dreams.

Studies[13] of older people show that one of the best predictors of happiness is whether a person considers his or her life to have a purpose. You can work all week, come home to eat and sleep and take up all sorts of hobbies, but if there isn't a reason for doing it, none of your activities will mean anything to you.

When you know where you are going you have a sense of purpose. And that sense of purpose gives you the motivation and energy you need to succeed. It is easier to apply ourselves to the activities we do when we know what we want and are able to see how what we are doing is making a difference. Say you are a student. Why should you study? To get your degree. So why do you care if you get a degree? Because you want to get a good job. Now the job may be many years away, but it is the motivation for all your efforts. Take away the outcome and the steps in between are just killing time.

So you need to think not only about what you want but why

you want it. You need to know what your purpose is before you can start to make it happen.

Write an Action Plan

Whatever your goals, an action plan can help you concentrate your energies. When you commit yourself in writing you take yourself much more seriously. Choose a short-term goal and write an action plan that will outline the methods used to achieve it and what your needs will be.

Start by stating your objective: 'I want to . . . '

Think about your method, the steps you will take to achieve your goals, the resources you will need, and give yourself a realistic deadline for reviewing your progress. Action plans for short-term goals will give you the self-confidence to plan for more far-reaching goals. Sometimes your plan won't work and you will have to revise it, but this doesn't matter. Action planning can help you see what your purpose is.

What if You Don't Know What You Want?

If you are not sure what you want, then you need to turn detective. Scientists everywhere notice patterns because they are looking for connections. In dealing with your emotions and happiness you need to be like a scientist. You need to notice patterns. Research shows[14] that those who are most likely to overcome unhappiness are those who can find out why they are unhappy and how it can be changed.

The more specific you are about defining your goals, the easier it is to achieve them. 'I want to be happy' isn't enough. You need to find out what exactly will make you happy. Here are some questions you need to ask yourself. What is prosperity for me? When will I feel happy about who I am and what I have created with my life? What goals am I striving for? What is my purpose?

What gives me joy? Lucky people are good at knowing what makes them happy. When they talk about their work or their life they are brimming with enthusiasm and motivation. Don't feel intimidated. You too can feel that way about your life. To create luck you need to work out what will make you happy and then know where to find it. You need to discover what gives you joy and what fills you with meaning and purpose.

What makes your heart sing?

Think about your emotions and happiness. What makes your heart sing? Bear in mind that what you may consider lucky may be a cause of unhappiness for someone else.

Do you think money is the answer? Why do many instant millionaires report that their money brings them more misery than joy? A study of life satisfaction[15] looked at twenty different factors that might contribute to happiness. Nineteen of these factors did matter, and one did not. The one factor that did not matter was financial status. Prosperity is not always related to how much money you have in the bank. Why are some people with less money happier than others who have more? Studies[16] show that what people like most about their work or chosen role in life isn't money or status but self-respect. Money is not the determining factor in happiness. Ask any young lover, first-time mother, or Olympic athlete.

> 'Riches are not from an abundance of worldly goods, but from a contented mind.' (Muhammad)

You may not have a clear idea of what you want, but you might know what you are most interested in: family, work, friends, or sport. That's the starting point. If, for example, you want to earn more money and be your own boss but aren't sure what the sensible starting point would be, go to meetings of self-employed people and talk to as many as you can to get a sense of what is required.

You might also want to take an evening class in something that has always interested you. The internet is a great place for information-gathering. If something fascinates you, write a letter to an expert, initiate a meeting with them, or buy a diary and start writing down all the things that you think will make you happy. Write down what you are best at and what other people compliment you on most, such as how organised you are or how you are such a laugh. After a day or so reread that diary. Think about the best moments in your life, the best holidays in your life. Do these have anything in common?

Plan dinner parties and invite people you don't know very well. Ask them questions about their lives and what they enjoy and what they want to do next. If you are very brave, ask them to picture you doing something with your life. What would it be? For one day, or one week even, avoid talking about yourself and ask people lots of questions about themselves.

One way to discover your hidden talents is to try something that seems unusual, offbeat, adventurous, or even silly. Plan an afternoon in which you do something you have never tried before, just because it sounds interesting, like going to a dancing class or having a full-body massage. Do some volunteer work, or take up an unusual hobby or part-time job. Draw up a business plan for something that just sounds like fun. Think about what you liked and disliked about it and how it surprised you. You never know what you might discover about yourself.

The point of these exercises is to make you step back from your life and see if there are any connections among the things you enjoy or feel energised by. When you listen to other people or try out new things, what really makes you feel excited? What are your strengths? Forget false modesty and think about what you are good at. You'll know you are on to something because you won't be able to stop thinking about it, and you will want to talk about it—except that other people might try to take it from you.

YOUR PERSONAL ADVISERS

One of the things lucky people tend to have is a personal advisory board they rely on for assistance. I don't mean mentors: I mean a mix of people who can offer a variety of viewpoints. They can include a former boss, a friend, the landlady who looked after you when you were between houses, your brother, your mother, and so on. These people can all offer advice when you need to make tough decisions. They can also help when you don't know what you want. They may see things that you miss or understand what you need better than you do. Why can others see what you can't? Because they have perspective along with a cool head and a fresh eye. This advice is given with a caution, though: you must choose your advisers well. There is nothing more disastrous than asking the wrong person for advice.

Jules Verne, having written a full-length play at sixteen years of age, gathered friends and family together to read his work to them. Their unexpected laughter prompted him to stop reading after the first act, and he later burnt the script. He went on to become one of the first science-fiction novelists and wrote *20,000 Leagues Under the Sea*, *Around the World in 80 Days*, and *A Journey to the Centre of the Earth*. He predicted the invention of aeroplanes, submarines, television, missiles, and space satellites.

Don't ask advice from people who don't really know you: colleagues at work, relatives who have a preconceived notion of who you are and what you need, friends who want to keep you right where you are, anyone with a grudge against you, anyone who will try to condone your attempts not to try. People you *can* ask for help are those who are willing to give you their time and listen to what you have to say. They don't constantly draw everything back to their experience, and they give their opinions carefully and thoughtfully.

If you are studying, reading, looking, listening, gathering information and considering your options and you still aren't sure what makes your heart sing, you could try looking into your past. Was there once something that made you happy but got left behind because you thought you had outgrown it?

> A friend of mine had a passion for horses when she was in her teens. After graduating she began a career in advertising. She quickly discovered that she hated her first job, and she started looking for another job. As she explored other opportunities she had a nagging sense that advertising wasn't for her. At one agency she was told that what they really needed was a research person to work on a new equestrian magazine. My friend's heart skipped a beat. This was exactly what she wanted.

Think about those dreams that you have always longed for but had to put aside because other things got in the way. Are you ready to go for them now? A change of scene may also help give you inspiration and new ideas.

Sometimes when you just don't have a clue what you want to do, you simply have to do something and stop dithering. If it doesn't work out, at least you will have learned about yourself from the experience.

You can never be sure of anything in life, and even if you do find something you love, you may find that as you get older your priorities change. Obviously, it's not very helpful to skip from interest to interest. If you don't commit yourself to something, you won't ever be good at it. But don't beat yourself up if you find that your interests and your passions change as you get older. Sometimes we just outgrow them and we need to find new goals to motivate and energise us all over again.

Expect to feel disappointed from time to time as you do your investigative work. Failure, time-wasting and loose ends are part of the luck-making process. But even experiences you thought were completely useless can turn out to have relevance several years later. Perhaps you started an art course only to find that you had absolutely no talent. But fast-forward a few years and the experience comes in handy when you are designing web sites or helping your children with their art work. To keep yourself from being discouraged, try to accept failure as part of the process, but also expect that sooner or later something good is bound to turn up. No experience is ever wasted if you learn something from it. Life works like that.

STILL NOT SURE? TRY SEEING GREEN

Only unlucky people become jealous and bitter about the good fortune of others. Envy is one of the most self-destructive emotions. But it can be useful too if you look at it calmly instead of falling into it blindly. Try this. The next time you feel a twinge of envy, don't ignore it or suppress it. Pay attention to how you are feeling. Ask yourself what these feelings are trying to tell you. Envy isn't a good place to end, but it can be a great place to start. It can help you see what you want.

> George felt the familiar pang of envy when his brother became a father for the third time. George wasn't in a relationship. His work commitments were heavy and he never had time to meet new people. What his feelings were telling him was not that he needed to become a father but that he needed to get more balance in his life.

If you feel uncertain about what you want, let feelings of envy point you in the direction of what you need. Sometimes you may not even be sure what it is you want until you see someone else with it and you wish it was yours. If you let envy work for you instead of against you, it can give you the energy and direction you need.

Sometimes envy can be hard to recognise. Have you ever felt angry, let down or annoyed by people who are doing well when you aren't? Rather than admit to being envious, you make negative comments like 'I couldn't care less' or 'It will all end in tears.' You may also notice that relationships change. When someone starts being cool towards you after being friendly, the chances are that one or both of you is envious and this is affecting your relationship.

Once you recognise envy, you are aware of what it is that someone else has that you want. You can turn things to your advantage by taking the focus off them and putting it on your needs. Make the envy about you, not about the other person. Remember, you are only in competition with yourself.

Ask yourself what it is about the other person's success that you really admire. Delve under the surface for the real thing you want. You may envy someone's figure. Is it the figure you want or the feeling of being sexier? A friend announces that she has a great home business idea. You rush home wishing you could steal her idea. Perhaps what you really want is very different. Are you reacting to someone who has the courage to follow her dreams, who can work at home and spend more time with her children?

Be careful not to let envy make you feel bitter and cheated. Don't think that because someone else has what you want, you can't have it because it is already taken. Get out of this kind of dog eat dog view. There is plenty of good luck in the world to go around.

Be realistic

When setting goals, there are a few things you need to bear in mind. The most important is, be bold, yet realistic. Even if anyone can be president of the United States, you probably need to take preparatory steps long before you wake up at fifty years of age with no political background. Although your goal must be realistic, make it interesting enough to excite you. There is no excitement in being mediocre or keeping up with the Joneses. Sometimes large goals are easier to accomplish than small ones. You may be astonished at what you can accomplish.

People who are lucky don't get everything they want, but they get most of what they want. In other words, they value what they know they can achieve. Unlucky people often set unattainable goals for themselves, setting themselves up to fail. The more realistic and attainable people's goals are, the more likely they are to feel happy about themselves.[17] Whether you are assessing your position at work or your relationship with your family, don't begin with fantasy pictures of the world's richest person or the world's ideal family. Stay with reality and strive to make things better, not perfect.

Align your goals

It is also important to align your goals to make sure they don't conflict with each other.

> Jack was a brilliant journalist. He travelled all over the world and loved to be in the thick of the action. But at the same time he missed his family dreadfully. For the past six months he had only spent two weekends with his daughters. Eventually he realised he could not keep his goal of being a dynamic reporter and being where he was needed most: with his children.

In a long-term study[18] over a period of ten years, life satisfaction was associated with consistency of life goals. Goals need to be consistent with one another to produce good results. Otherwise you're just struggling against yourself—a sure recipe for becoming unlucky.

Diversify your goals

Set your sights on being generally content and not on every aspect of your life being perfect. One experiment[19] showed that happiness was greater among those whose lives were generally positive in many areas that mattered to them. You wouldn't invest all your money in one company, would you? So don't invest all your happiness in one person, company, project, or promotion. Diversify your hopes. Don't pin your hopes on getting a promotion and end up ruining a happy home life. Don't define your life according to your relationship and end up feeling devastated if there are problems with that relationship. Build your hopes on the many things that matter to you.

Research[20] on a large group of students showed that those who were less likely to link their attainment of a specific goal to their general mood were more likely to feel satisfied. We tend to be happier when all the pieces in our life are in good shape than when one that we care about is perfect and the rest are falling apart. Absolute happiness does not exist, because there is always room for improvement. Those who understand this can appreciate what they have. Those who cannot accept this can never appreciate what they have, even if their circumstances improve.

Enjoy the many aspects of your life. With varied options, you're more likely to get lucky in some of them.

KEEP YOUR GOALS FLEXIBLE

Don't fixate on the idea that there is only one perfect thing you should do or one perfect place to live. Successful people know there may well be many things they could do and that it is fine to throw themselves into things without worrying about whether something else might be better. They also know that success may result from something they least expect.

> Donald Fisher was a real-estate developer in the late 1960s. He became frustrated when he tried to exchange a pair of Levi jeans for a different size at a San Francisco department store. On a whim, he opened a shop specialising in jeans,

> called Gap, which has become one of the most successful speciality chains in retailing history.

Stay focused but flexible in your goal-setting. Sometimes opportunities present themselves in the least expected ways, and you may find yourself changing direction. If you approach everything you do with an attitude of positive expectancy and enthusiasm, sooner or later you will settle on the right thing for you.

And remember not to confuse the means with the end. For example, if you want a fancy car, the car is the means, not the end. You want a car because of how it will make you feel when you get it. If you can recognise that it is not the thing that you want but the feelings associated with it, then you increase your chances of luck. A car may make you feel good, but lots of other things can do that too. Why limit yourself to one?

Busy is best

Studies[21] of students show that those who have more to do often feel more motivated. Despite having the more demanding schedule, the students didn't feel more stressed than those who did less. Lucky people may often complain they have too much to do, but this problem is far preferable to having too little to do. Ask any out-of-work dancer, actor, musician, or writer.

Busy is good but, remember, being stressed isn't. The constant urge to accomplish more, to do better, is a marked characteristic of those who want to attract good luck; but don't over-commit yourself. If your list of 'I've been meaning to do' is too long, decide what you are going to do and cross the other items off. Work towards those things you really want and declare that you can't do the remainder because your resources are limited. By being selective you will probably notice an increased energy, a clarity of mind and a stronger desire to achieve what you specifically plan on doing.

Go for the goal

And when you have chosen reasonable, meaningful and aligned goals, go after them with all your heart. In the words of the great Jedi master, 'Do or do not. There is no try.' Would you lend money to someone who said, 'I'll try to return it'? Would you get married to a partner who said 'I'll try' instead of 'I do'? If you know what you want to do, start taking steps towards your goal. Reach for the stars, take a risk, and act. Have you an unfulfilled dream? a burning ambition? a creative idea?

> 'Whatever you can do or dream you can, begin it. Boldness has genius, power and magic in it.' (Goethe)

If so, imagine yourself doing it. Unless you allow your mind to absorb these pictures, you'll never do them. Put your plan into action and give it all you've got. Invest every ounce of skill and energy to achieve it.

And once you achieve a goal, rest awhile and set another. The business of life is to go forward. Think of your life as an exciting journey where you are on a quest for your own unlimited potential. Success is a journey, not a destination. Many people find that reaching for a goal is more rewarding than actually achieving it. You don't have to attain your goal to enjoy it. The fun starts now.

Ask for what you want

Once you know the direction in which you are headed, the next important step is to single out those people who can help you. If you want something to happen you must dare to ask for what you want. This could involve being ridiculed, rejected, or ignored, but if you never take a risk you will never get what you want.

And when you ask for something, say what you mean. This may seem obvious, but we don't always say what we mean. Next time you don't get what you want, check that you asked for it clearly. If you tell someone you are fine while in fact you are angry, you can't expect them to be mind-readers and know what you are really thinking. Say exactly what you mean and ask for what you want. If your partner asks you what you want for your birthday, tell him or her. Don't pretend not to care. If you want to go to a cinema and your friend wants to go shopping, tell her what you would like to do and then work out a compromise. Not only will your feelings of self-respect increase but you will have a much better chance of getting what you want.

Your luck network

We talked about networking in the last chapter. Now it's time to give some focus to your networking. List the names, fax and phone number of every influential person in your chosen field with whom you are remotely friendly. Many big breaks come from the least likely contacts. You may know many people who can introduce you to others who can help you.

You may have resisted keeping in touch with key people for fear it would be seen as begging for favours. Get over it. Luck, success and happiness require openness and honesty both ways. Luck's gatekeepers are often happy to help—if you create the right impression (see chapter 10).

When you start getting in touch with people it's best to fax or write before you phone, unless you are on very friendly terms. Be brief and respectful in your correspondence, and most people will be happy to help you. The best time to make contact is early in the morning, before it starts to get busy. More people answer their phones then and are more receptive to listening to you. If you wait until later you are more likely to reach voice mail or assistants.

When writing letters, open the letter with a sincere compliment, keep your tone upbeat, and perhaps even suggest a meeting: breakfast or lunch is best. Perhaps start by asking the person to give you the names of a few contacts who would be helpful. When these contacts help you out, be sure to let your gatekeeper know about it. Once a gatekeeper hears that he or she gave you a contact that was helpful, they are more likely to offer you other names or assistance.

Once your gatekeeper gives you the names of people to call, set out to obtain at least two names from each of them. Then you get contacts from those contacts, and so on. Once you have a list of names, suggest a meeting. Make sure you thank each contact before you move forward, otherwise you will leave a bad impression, and that will cause you bad luck.

You become lucky by allowing your sincerity, honesty and enthusiasm to shine through and attract others to help you achieve your goals. It isn't about using people. If you approach them in the right manner, successful people won't be offended if you ask for advice or help. They understand that this is the way the world works. And, who knows? One day you may be in a position to help them.

Let's do lunch

> Remember the lucky person's rule: people who don't talk are always considered the best conversationalists. Listen carefully and ask relevant questions. Especially, ask your gatekeeper for advice. This will make them feel good. It is flattering to be considered an expert and to know that someone wants to seek out our wisdom. This also sets the stage for your gatekeeper to become a mentor.

Do you deserve luck?

Let's say you've found out what excites you, you've set your goal, you've made your action plan, and you're doing great at asking for help in carrying it out. Success is just around the corner! And suddenly all you have worked for starts to crumble and you say your luck has finally run out.

> 'It's the story of my life,' says Larry. 'I always nearly make it. Everything goes really well, and then it all starts to slip away. I can't tell you how many times I have lost the perfect contract at the last moment. I suddenly start to doubt myself and wonder if I am really good enough. I miss a deadline and then another and another, and before I know it I've lost a client.'

If you don't think you deserve luck, the incongruity between who you think you are and what you can achieve may cause you to fail when you should succeed. If you are one of those people who sabotages their own success, it is crucial that you resolve to change the pattern. It won't be easy. You may need counselling or therapy to wrestle with your demons or ingrained childhood patterns, or you may need to hire a life coach to change those self-defeating behaviour patterns that are not promoting success.

The most important thing, though, is to work on your self-esteem. We touched on this in part 1, and you might want to go back at this point. If at the core you believe you are a loser, you will end up sabotaging results that conflict with your perception of yourself.

Stop self-sabotaging behaviour

You may wonder why anyone would be so stupid as to destroy their own chances of success. It's probably because most of our self-sabotaging behaviour is intended to protect us from pain and suffering. But ultimately these choices bring unhappiness and bad luck.

The first step is to become aware of your own behaviour and choices. Begin to notice when you are doing things that do not promote positive results, and take responsibility for how you are contributing to problems in your life. Start thinking about what your self-sabotaging habits are in all areas of life. What triggers them? What are you gaining from them?

Secondly, build a new, positive identity for yourself, one that matches the results that you want to create in your work. This means catching negative statements and replacing them with more factual statements that allow the possibility of change. 'I am no good at anything' can be replaced with 'I have habits that don't bring me success.' The second statement is just a simple fact—without that weight of self-blame. Always remind yourself that you are not your behaviour.

Thirdly, concentrate on the positive rather than the negative. If all you say is negative, 'I don't want this' or 'I hate that' or 'This is wrong' or 'What a joke!' it is impossible to think about what you do want. And don't beat yourself up about past mistakes. There is always a positive side to disappointment and failure. We all make mistakes, but no mistake is ever wasted. How else would you ever learn what you don't want? Mistakes are all lessons that can help you discover what you want.

DON'T THINK 'WHAT IF'

> Research[22] on Olympic athletes found that those who spent the least time thinking about things that might have ended differently were the most satisfied with their experience. Spending your time thinking about what might have been if you had changed things is counterproductive and unlucky. Think about how you can improve in the future, and don't waste the present thinking about how you might have changed the past.

FORGET AFFIRMATIONS: THEY DON'T WORK

You may have read here or there about the benefits of positive affirmations. It is said that if you tell yourself enough times how beautiful, talented and clever you are, these things will be yours. Sounds easy, doesn't it? There's only one problem. Affirmations don't work. Here's why. If you unconsciously believe that you don't deserve something, or it's selfish or greedy to ask, or if you aren't prepared to do the work required to obtain it, you'll be contradicting yourself. Every time you try to say yes, another part of you will say no. You can try to silence the negative internal voice, but it just shouts louder. The affirmation that was supposed to lift your spirit starts to drag you down. And if nothing changes in your life, then you start to believe that you really are a failure.

If you want to do affirmations, make sure you affirm clear goals that are within reason. You can always be open to luck for the miraculous to happen, but don't assume it will. Express clearly that you believe your goal is possible to achieve and you are ready to receive it. Be optimistic but also realistic that things will work out for the best and you will get what you want and need. Anchor your affirmations in reality and they will lift your spirits; anchor them in fantasy and they will drag you down.

Have your cake and eat it too

Having the courage and willingness to claim what you want is a major element in a lucky life. This may be hard for you if you have spent most of your life settling for what you don't want. Taking the step from mediocrity to quality will require conviction. Decide right now that when opportunity comes your way you won't hesitate. You will seize the moment.

Lucky people not only have their cake, they eat it too, and they savour every delicious bite! They don't need a sense of crisis to feel alive: they can take time off between goals to rest and renew; they don't feel undeserving of their success. They allow themselves to enjoy their success.

Savour, really savour your every accomplishment, however small. Give yourself a pat on the back if it is deserved. Smile inwardly at those who said you would never pull it off. Reward yourself with gifts or experiences you enjoy. When someone congratulates you, resist the urge to qualify your success with 'yes buts' and apologies; simply say, 'Thank you.'

If things aren't going as well as you hoped, ride out these feelings and rediscover the hidden benefits and advantages you may not have noticed before. Spend time with partners or friends you may have ignored a little in pursuit of your goals. Don't feel bad about spending time watching, listening, daydreaming. You need time to refresh and renew yourself. Find a corner you call your own, and use it to read, write, and imagine.

Every day leave yourself some time to enjoy, be silly, and laugh. Regularly having fun is one of the most important factors for a lucky life. Research[23] shows that people who spend time having fun are more likely to feel happy about themselves and their lives. And, finally, know that you pulled off your victory not through luck but because you planned it and worked for it, and you can do it again in a different arena and under different circumstances if you want to. Remind yourself that you are the one who sets your goals, the one who can make things happen in your life. Congratulate yourself on recognising your power to change your life.

Actions to take today to get what you want

1. Without being unrealistic (if you want to be a ballet dancer and you're thirty-eight years old without any training it is pretty obvious that you should aspire towards something else), ask yourself what it is you want. Think about how you will look and feel and behave when you have what you want. Naming what you truly want means you can begin to direct your life, because you have a goal that is exactly, precisely and specifically identified.

2. Need help finding a goal? What was the most satisfying enjoyable time in your life? As children we all had dreams of what we'd like to be when we grew up. What was your dream? What would make you feel happy now? What lights you up when you do it? Many lucky people find that writing down

their goals really helps. Writing forces you to be specific, which is very important in goal-setting.

3. If you could spend an hour with one person who ever lived, who would that person be, and why?

4. Visualise your funeral. Who would be there? What would they remember you for? You will be amazed how quickly this exercise can organise your thoughts about what you do and do not want to happen in your life.

5. Create something. Reawaken your interest and motivation by creating something. Decide upon a project, however small, and go ahead and be creative. It could be writing a letter to someone you care about, planting some flowers, taking some photographs—the possibilities are endless. It's amazing how quickly your interest in life can be recaptured when you encourage yourself to be creative.

6. Write down self-defeating habits—overeating, drinking, worrying—that are stopping you from achieving your goals. Rather than thinking 'poor me' or blaming someone or something else, such as your parents or your job, step outside your behaviour and question it. Develop an inner witness who will remind you that you are doing things that will not make you feel happy, and take responsibility for changing them by building a new, positive identity for yourself, one that matches the results you want to create.

7. Many people tend to feel threatened by those who appear to be more successful and so choose to spend time with people who are not as successful as they are themselves. Check your motives. If you spend your time with people who cannot handle success, you may end up being just like them. Look for

people who have themselves made a success of whatever you are trying to achieve, and learn from them. Success attracts success, just as negativity attracts negativity. Mix with people you admire, and you will feel inspired to create your own success.

8. Make a list of all the people who might be in a position to offer advice, give you contacts, or help you get where you want to go in some way. Depending on how familiar you are with them, make contact either by conversation, letter, e-mail, fax, or phone.

9. Every week schedule some time for fun into your diary: an afternoon with your children, a trip to the cinema with your friends, a night out at the theatre. Whatever it is, make sure you are never too busy, too preoccupied or too fixated on your goals to miss out on fun and laughter.

9

Get Time on Your Side

Learning when to be patient, when to persist, when to quit and when to pounce aren't all there is to secret number 3. The other half is learning how to manage your time.

Keyword: Adaptability

Sometimes it is futile to fight reality. Have you ever tried really hard to be on time for something and yet still arrived late?

However goal-oriented, well prepared and motivated you are, you can't control everything that happens to you. However many things you do to increase your chances of luck in life, there will always be accidents and unforeseen circumstances that throw you off course. During those times you need to be flexible enough to go where life is taking you—which may not be the way you originally intended.

When unexpected things happen to you, what do you do? Do you become agitated over things you have no control over? Or do you shrug your shoulders and adapt to the situation? Psychologists at the University of Michigan found that although goals are important, they can be damaging if they are not flexible. If your goals are incompatible with your abilities, your goals will increase the likelihood of unhappiness.[24]

> Steven set himself the goal of buying a house for his young family before he was twenty-five. He saved as much as he could, but it wasn't enough to get a mortgage approval. He

took on a second job and then a third. He worked himself sick and began to resent his wife and family. Instead of living a happy life and saving for a house one day, he allowed his rigid goals to end up harming his life.

Sometimes you start working for what you want but things don't go according to plan. When this happens to lucky people they know how to improvise. As we saw in the last chapter, you have to let your goals evolve with your life circumstances. It is important to update your goals over time as you consider your changing priorities and resources.

Discovering hidden treasures

Lucky people aren't rigid and fixed in their actions or viewpoints. They have goals, but they know how to adapt along the way to let luck in. This is a good thing. Take a look at your life. Aren't you glad you didn't always get what you thought you wanted? Is there something or some person that you weren't looking for that came to you by surprise and is now the biggest blessing of your life? What about that relationship you thought was perfect but in retrospect clearly wasn't right for you? Many times when we think we are headed somewhere else, fate has a way of changing our plans. We get what we want in the most unexpected of ways.

> Warren Buffet, an Omaha billionaire, built his fortune over a lifetime of shrewd investments. Throughout his teens he planned to join the Harvard Business School when he was twenty. The day he got the rejection letter from Harvard he was disappointed but immediately started researching other business schools. It wasn't until then that he noticed that Benjamin Graham and David Dodd, whose book *Security Analysis* he so admired, both taught at Columbia. He applied at the last minute and was accepted. There he got to know Graham, who became his mentor and boss.

> Buffett once told the magazine *Fortune* that when he looks back on it now, 'Probably the luckiest thing that ever happened to me was being rejected by Harvard.'

Try not to be rigid about your plans or to get frustrated when unexpected disappointments occur. If something in your life isn't going according to your plan, remind yourself that we live in a world of surprises and there may be something around the corner you just don't know about. For every loss there can be a gain. There will be times when the door of opportunity seems to slam shut in your face, but don't despair. Alexander Graham Bell had the answer for this: 'When one door closes, another opens, but we often look so long and regretfully upon the closed door we do not see the ones which open for us. So alter your course and move on.'

Patience

How often have you heard people say about meeting their loved one, 'I gave up looking and then he or she showed up'? Lots of people miss out on good luck because they aren't patient enough to wait for it. They want quick fixes and easy-come fortune. But sometimes the most important thing you can do to bring good luck into your life is to bide your time. This isn't the same as giving up or being lazy. It is about waiting until the moment is right.

Patience isn't passively waiting for some impossible miracle: it is recognising that sometimes in life the most important thing you can do to attract luck is to move on to something else that inspires you, and let the other dream simmer for a while. You trust that it will come to you when the time is right, and in the meantime you get busy with other luck-making schemes. Taking action may be the last thing you should do right now. By letting some time go by without trying to make something happen, you may eventually get what you want.

Sometimes luck happens not when you are not trying to make it happen but when you are simply open and available to what shows up. Hold a bird too tight in your hand and you crush it. You need to give luck room to breathe. Inspiration often comes when you are in a semi-conscious, relaxed state. Work hard, and if things are not going your way, keep hoping and believing luck will happen, but stop trying to force it to happen. Hang in there long enough, so that when the time is right for other people to see things your way, you are ready and willing to act.

Impatience is dangerous. A fine dinner takes time to season and cook, and the same applies to maximising your chances of luck. Hopeful patience is a luck-making attitude. It's not giving up on your goal. It's recognising that you can move forward towards your goal even if you are not actively working on it but in the meantime are taking care of other things in your life.

Tomorrow is another day

When life doesn't go as planned, sometimes it is best to chalk it up as a rough day. What you can't solve now you may be able to solve tomorrow. Things always look better after a good night's sleep. Many small problems go away by themselves, and you shouldn't waste time worrying about them. Most lucky people understand this concept. They don't get stressed about what doesn't need to be solved immediately. When decisions need to be made they let their emotions cool first. Or they say they will get right on it but let a little time pass so that emotional heat has had time to burn out.

Giving problems time to work themselves out also helps you avoid stress. You need to be detached and at ease so that you can exercise good judgment and make solid decisions. No problem is so important that it has to be resolved right this minute. Don't let other people convince you otherwise. Consider the problem from all angles, and take your time. Learn to relax. When the going gets rough, tell yourself to slow down.

HANDLING IMPATIENCE

Patience isn't a popular virtue today. We live in a fast-paced world. We want fast food, fast fun, and fast living. But impatience is the enemy of luck. It gets you stressed and alienates other people.

We all exaggerate our needs and wants at times. The key to handling your impatience is in the way you talk to yourself. Look at your choice of words. Are you exaggerating? Do you think there is only one way you can be happy? Do you really have to have everything now in order to be happy?

When you are in an impatient, angry or desperate state you can't create luck. Remove your tendency to exaggerate and you will begin to feel more relaxed. It also helps to believe that, even though things aren't going well right now, something better lies ahead.

BELIEVE THERE IS SOMETHING BETTER IN STORE FOR YOU

A good motivation for developing greater patience when the going gets tough is to think of all the times in your life when changes of plan or unexpected surprises worked out well and you found yourself saying, 'Isn't it well we didn't do that. This is so much better.' It's often the case that what eventually shows up is better than what you had to let go. Think about all the things you have in your life right now that were not planned but that turned out well: an unplanned pregnancy, an unexpected job offer, a relocation you despised but that worked out for the best, the end of a relationship and the beginning of another, better one.

When things don't go according to plan, rather than giving up, concentrate your energies with positive expectation for the future and believe that there must be something better in store for you. Rather than becoming frustrated about the loss of what you planned for, get excited about the possibility of better plans. If things don't turn out as hoped, believe that you are being steered in another direction—although you don't know what it is yet—and that if you remain open and willing to find it, it will show up.

Let the pieces come together

When you feel like giving up, think of your life as a giant jigsaw puzzle that has to come together before you receive the luck you deserve. You may be desperate for something to happen now, or you don't understand why things aren't working out as planned, but nothing is going to make sense until all the pieces of your life come together at the right time.

> Elton John struggled as a member of several unsuccessful rock groups in the 1960s, and his first single, 'Come Back Baby', never made the charts. He failed an audition for Liberty Records, and in 1968 his debut album, *Empty Skies*, flopped. Elton John eventually became the most successful pop artist of the seventies, best known for his albums *Madman across the Water, Goodbye Yellow Brick Road, Captain Fantastic and Brown Dirt Cowboy*. His hit songs include 'Rocket Man', 'Candle in the Wind', 'Don't Let the Sun go Down on Me', and 'I Guess That's Why They Call It the Blues'.

When to cut your losses

Sometimes when your plans are detoured or taking longer than you would like, you have to be patient; but luck-making is also knowing when to cut your losses and move on so that you can create luck in some other way.

Have you ever bought a pair of shoes that needed breaking in to become comfortable? You persevere for six months, but they still hurt like hell. You now have two choices: you can keep trying, or you can decide to get rid of them. There is a big difference between shoes that fit and shoes that are the wrong size. They aren't going to fit, however hard you try. The same could be said for a relationship, a job, or a church, and so on.

Hanging on for too long can be deadly as far as luck-making is concerned. What are you putting up with that you shouldn't be right now? What mistakes have you made that can be remedied only by acknowledging that it is time to move on? Success and failure can only be interpreted over time. You may find that your biggest failure is the event that propels you to success, but only if you move on.

WHEN TO BE PERSISTENT AND WHEN TO QUIT

How do you know when to be patient and when to quit? This is where intuition comes in, and we'll explore that later.

Try asking yourself if quitting too early or staying too long in something is a pattern for you. Do you need to persevere or to leave? Is your present situation draining your energy? If you weren't focusing on this, what would you be doing instead? What do you have to lose if you stay? What do you have to lose if you move on? Which is worse?

If you are doing the same thing over and over again and things are still not working, it is time to reflect. When confronting a problem we often try to solve it in the same way over and over again, getting more and more frustrated with each failure. We get angry, try even harder, exert even more energy, and try to force the same solution we tried before. Sometimes we get so frustrated that we abandon the task altogether and try to convince ourselves that it wasn't worth having anyway.

Certainly trying harder can pay off at times, but more often it might be appropriate to back off, detach yourself for a while, so you can think of other ways to achieve the task. Stop trying so hard to make it happen. Often when you relax for a while and listen to your inner voice a different path opens up and emerges more clearly. You may even find that your run of bad luck is actually the best thing that could have happened. Sometimes things happen that appear at first to be unfortunate but later turn out to be good luck after all.

The right moment doesn't exist

Luck-making is not just about knowing when to be patient and when to quit. It is also about knowing when to pounce.

If an opportunity presents itself, behave like a lucky person and grab it. Worry later about whether you seemed pushy, inappropriate, or too eager. There is no such thing as the right time. If you wait until you feel you deserve it or you feel ready, that time may never come. Try this shortcut. Get a hair-cut that makes you feel great and clothes that are wonderful to wear. The next time a fabulous opportunity hovers nearby, for example if you see the man or woman of your dreams, or you bump into someone who may be able to help you, don't let it slip by. Pounce.

Be ready to grab good luck even if it happens before you are fully prepared. Sometimes you have to jump before you feel ready. Unlucky people are afraid of making mistakes and looking silly. They wonder what the best way is and how they can get themselves ready. Lucky people, by contrast, seize the moment. To improve your chances of luck you need to stop thinking and just get out there. Send that application, write that novel, start that business, ask the man or woman of your dreams out for a date, book that holiday, and so on. Do your groundwork by all means, but then get off your backside and have a go.

Be creative with the rules

There is truth in the saying that rules are made to be broken. Lucky people don't always start at the beginning and wait for the appropriate moment. They don't always follow what is perceived to be the correct way of doing things. This doesn't mean they are dishonest or disruptive—later you will see that acting in any way that isn't honest and sincere is an enemy of luck; it means they use the rules creatively.

Don't automatically assume that you need training simply because it is the obvious thing to do. There isn't always one perfect way of doing things. When lucky people are offered an opportunity, do you think they say, 'I haven't done that before. I haven't been trained. Maybe I should get a degree first'? Of course they don't. Sometimes you need to work your way up the ladder to get what you want, but sometimes you don't. Look for shortcuts that might allow you entry higher up. Is there someone you know or something you could do that can lift you up? Bending the so-called rules can be beneficial.

If you are being told that you aren't ready for something, don't be content with that timetable. Sometimes it is better to strike before the iron is hot! Before you take anyone's advice to wait and see, ask yourself what you are actually waiting for and why.

I'm sure that lucky people who get what they want have been told over and over again to slow down. But through trial and error they discover that sometimes if you slow down and follow the rules you don't get anywhere.

> There was a man who had one dream: to become an actor. He just needed a part to play, but nobody would give him one. So he decided to write his own part. He put together a script, and looked for someone to produce it. He went from agent to agent, studio to studio, but nobody was interested. He was turned down a thousand times, but still he persisted. Everybody told him to give it a rest, try something else, or accept that it wasn't going to happen. He didn't listen. Finally, someone liked his script and offered him $100,000 for it. He turned it down, because they wanted someone else to play his part. He kept searching until he got exactly what he wanted. He eventually starred in the film he wrote and won an Oscar. It was then followed by four sequels. For holding on to his dream and turning down the initial $100,000 offer he can now command several million dollars a picture.
>
> What would have happened if Sylvester Stallone had

> listened to everyone's advice, followed the rules, and slowed down? Nobody would ever have known who Rocky was.

Warning: If you do decide to bend the rules a little, do it in a luck-making way (see chapter 11).

Stop making excuses

Backing off for a while when something isn't working or rethinking your approach isn't the same as using patience as an excuse not to make changes that are needed. Your mind will present you with all sorts of excuses for not moving forward with your life. Inaction keeps you stuck in a stifling prison until something dramatic happens to motivate you. Have you ever noticed how motivated people become when they are told they have a terminal illness? Don't wait for that shock.

> In one year Anthony Burgess finished five novels. What motivated him was being told he had only six months to live. He had no money to leave to his wife, and this was his only resource for leaving any kind of security for his family.
>
> But Anthony Burgess did not die. His cancer went into remission and then disappeared. In his long and full life he wrote seventy books. Without the death sentence from cancer at the age of forty he may never have written anything.

You don't need a death sentence to start doing the things you have always wanted to do with your life. You can do them all right now. List five things you would do differently in the next six months if you thought you had only a year to live. If you are finding it hard to break from routine, don't try to change everything at once. Do just one thing differently, and as you start feeling refreshed this will motivate you to further action.

SEEK OPPORTUNITY

Don't wait for opportunity to find you. Seek it out. Lucky people are not necessarily more talented than anyone else, but they usually get what they want, because they seek opportunities, not guarantees. They don't wait for incentives and are constantly alert to what is going on around them. Lucky people know that every situation holds the seed of opportunity, and when it appears they are prepared to seize it and act on it. For lucky people, every day is potentially full of golden opportunities.

> To appreciate the value of a year, ask a student who failed an exam.
> To appreciate the value of one month, ask the mother of a premature baby.
> To realise the value of one week, ask the editor of a weekly magazine.
> To realise the value of one day, ask the self-employed builder who has five children to feed.
> To realise the value of one hour, ask the lovers who long to meet.
> To realise the value of one minute, ask the person who missed a train.
> To realise the value of one second, ask the person who survived an accident.
> To realise the value of a millisecond, ask the person who won a silver medal at the Olympics.

MANAGE YOUR TIME

Getting time on your side also means learning how to manage your time. In the last chapter you decided what was important to you. Now you need to organise your time so that your priorities come first in your life. You may have goals and intentions, but putting them first is often the hard part. Rather like packing a suitcase, the better you organise your life, the better you'll be able to pack everything in: more time for yourself, family, friends, work, and your goals.

PUT FIRST THINGS FIRST

We live in a 'now' society: everything is urgent. The trouble with this is that urgent things often have the appearance of being important even when they're not. For example, a ringing phone is urgent, but it may only be a telemarketer on the other end. Pay attention to what's truly important, and don't get sidetracked by the almost urgent. Procrastinators are addicted to urgency, both important and unimportant. They put things off until they become a crisis. But they like it that way. Their minds don't kick into gear until there is urgency. Everything is done at the last possible minute, and the result of too much time spent in crisis is stress, burn-out, and mediocre performance.

If you are one of those people who find it hard to say no, your life will be littered with activities that are important to other people but not to you. You'd like to say no but are afraid of offending. The comedian Bill Cosby once said, 'I don't know the key to success but I know the key to failure is to try and please everybody.' There is a difference between helping other people and being taken for a ride.

Then there are people who concentrate on things that are neither urgent nor important. If these people enjoy things, they do them to excess, like sleeping, watching television, using the internet, talking on the phone, and shopping. They just love to hang out. All these things are part of a healthy life-style, but when they are done to excess they become a waste of time. You know when you cross the line. You eat a few chocolates and they taste delicious; you eat the whole box and you feel sick.

Lucky people are not procrastinators, 'yes' people, or slackers: they set priorities. They take a look at everything they have to do and then put first things first and last things last. Although it is a struggle, staying balanced is important. They take time to refresh and renew themselves. They avoid stress and burn-out by working for things in advance. People that matter come first. They know how to say no. When a friend invites them for a drink and they have an important interview the next day they say, 'No, thanks; but how about tomorrow night?'

Decide what is important to you, and put that at the top of your list. When urgent things crop up, deal with them only if they are important too. Decide what matters to you and what you will and will not do. Think through what the commitment will take, what the best possible schedule will be, and what you should say yes to and no to. And then be very firm and stick to your decision.

If you are addicted to crises, try doing important things a little earlier. If you always say yes, start saying no a little more often. Remember, when you say no you are saying yes to more important things. And if you just want to hang around, don't stop being relaxed and chilled out: just do it a little less often.

DEVELOP DISCIPLINE

In the words of Frank A. Clark in *The Country Parson*, 'It's hard to detect good luck. It looks so much like something you have earned.' Lucky people finish what they start, even if it means doing things they don't always like in order to reach their goals. Lucky people have discipline. It takes discipline to overcome your fears; it takes discipline to be strong in the hard moments and resist peer pressure; it takes discipline to meet deadlines and commitments; and it takes discipline to be patient and work hard.

Psychologists spend years studying successful people to find out the key ingredient that made them successful. What do you think they found? Successful people are willing to do things they don't always like to do, because they know these things will lead them to their goals. Research[25] on adults has revealed that a tendency to be disciplined, deliberate and patient has a positive effect on happiness. In other words, discipline helps you get things done whether you feel like it or not. Do you think a footballer enjoys every hour of practice every day? Does a person who is working their way through university enjoy their second job?

Most of us like to stay in our comfort zones. But if you want to increase your chances of luck you have to take risks and do things that may make you feel uncomfortable. This will almost certainly involve hard work and dedication, and sometimes you will need to ask yourself whether or not you value something enough to be willing to continue even if it hurts. Are you willing to forgo some temporary pleasures or conveniences in order to achieve your goals?

Margaret Thatcher once said, 'I wasn't lucky. I deserved it.' Creating luck in life often correlates with how disciplined and committed you are to doing what it takes to get what you want—even if you don't like it. For example, if you want your partner to be happy, you may need to learn to compromise. If you want your children to be happy, you need to give them your time. If you want money, you have to go to work to earn it. If you want to stay healthy, you need to keep fit and eat well.

You may well find that this quality of lucky people is the hardest one to live by. So don't get discouraged if you struggle. You are not alone. There are many ways whereby you can help yourself develop discipline to do what it takes to create luck in your life. Some of them were mentioned earlier. Here are some strategies that can help.

- Keep your ego in check. Don't wait until you are better at doing things until you do them. Have a go now.
- Make yourself accountable to someone else. Find someone with whom you can communicate regularly about your progress.
- Be a good role model for your loved ones. Do you want your children or family to learn laziness or luck-making from you?
- Set small goals first, and let the sense of achievement when they are successfully completed motivate you to take further action.

- Set regular times for reviewing the situation. If you are struggling don't give up, but wait until you reach your review date. Then assess how you can improve the situation.

More time management tips

A tidy office or household is important. If you are organised you are efficient, and efficiency is the key to taking control of your time and generating good luck. Also, a clean environment makes you feel good and makes those who visit you feel good. An untidy place reduces self-respect and other people's respect for you and your work.

Tips for making the most of your time

- Start delegating tasks that eat up your creative thinking time.
- Throw out things when you don't need them any more.
- Get a filing system that works.
- Get rid of junk.
- Return phone calls in the afternoon and use the morning for brainwork.
- Allocate priorities to work as it comes in.
- Avoid distractions.
- Seek out only the people you need to see.
- Hire smart people to do what you don't want to worry about. If you are not in a position to do this, concentrate on what you like to do, and avoid taking on projects that will distract you.

Set a household routine

You may feel overwhelmed by household chores that need doing regularly: the kitchen needs cleaning, the sitting-room needs vacuuming, the lawn needs to be mowed, and lots of other things need doing. If you set up a reasonable schedule you won't be facing an endless list of chores. With a routine you won't waste time wondering what is next.

Studies of families[26] have shown that routines in households improve feelings of satisfaction.

If you have lots of tasks to complete, set an order so you don't start one thing, get distracted by something else, and feel as if you haven't accomplished anything. When you have a routine you finish what you start, and every step of the way you see that you are closer to being finished.

Get a diary

You don't need to get a high-tech Palm Pilot: just a small diary is all you need. Remember that a planner isn't meant to restrict you but to free you. You no longer have to worry about forgetting things or double-booking yourself. You can keep all your important information in one place.

Take some time each week to plan the week ahead. Think about what you would like to complete that week. Be realistic and think in concrete terms. You need to be able to measure things and know that they are improving. You might set as your goals: I want to finish this task an hour faster; I want to have dinner with my family every night; I want to make this task more cost-effective. These goals come with built-in directions. These are goals you can work towards and successfully complete. Research[27] shows that feelings of confidence and satisfaction increase significantly with concrete thinking.

Block out time in your diary for your goals. That way everyday activities can fit around them. Once you have scheduled your important activities you can write in all the other little to-do's, daily tasks and appointments. Try your best to follow your plan as the week progresses; but if you don't get everything accomplished don't beat yourself up. Even if you achieve only one out of five things you will have accomplished more than you might have without a plan.

And if you feel frustrated that you can't remember things, write them down in your diary. Research shows that people who feel that their best ideas escape them are less likely to feel content than those who don't.[28] Good ideas come floating into our heads and will just as easily float out. Writers often carry a notebook around with them to hold on to fleeting thoughts. Keeping a diary or notebook will help you feel more in control of your life.

Get time on your side

Does this time management thing really work? Yes. You can't recycle wasted time. Treasure every moment. Give priority to what is important to you. Draw up a schedule with attainable goals. If you want to make luck happen, you can't do it without time on your side.

Take action today to get time on your side

1. Are you worn out and exhausted? Are you pursuing your goals but not getting anywhere? Are you afraid to stop because you worry you'll never get what you want? If you are, take a break and do something different right now: book a holiday, make plans to see friends, go shopping, read a novel, think about something else.

2. Tell yourself that nothing is so important that you have to resolve it now. Take your time. Sleep on it. If other people are trying to make you resolve it, let them wait. Give problems time to work themselves out. Wait until you feel detached and at ease and have examined every angle so that you can make good judgments and solid decisions.

3. When good luck does strike, many of us want to go back in time. 'Why couldn't I have done this sooner? I'm happy now, but why did I waste my teens and twenties feeling miserable?' It doesn't work that way. If you had the good fortune earlier, it wouldn't have been the perfect timing that it is now. You wouldn't have appreciated it then. What makes you content

now might have made you miserable if it had come earlier. You simply weren't ready. It's happening to you now because you can handle it. You have also learned from the difficulties you experienced. Think of three things that make you feel good now. What were you doing before these things arrived that you needed to learn first? Why was the timing of these events perfect?

4. Have you been resting for quite some time and now need to get moving? Take small action steps to demonstrate to yourself that you are ready to take action again to get what you want.

5. Is quitting too early a pattern for you? Do you need to learn to stick at it? Have you a pattern of staying too long on something that isn't working for you? Do you need to leave?

6. Make a list of five necessary but unpleasant tasks you have been putting off. Put a completion date on each task. Complete each task. Immediate action on unpleasant projects reduces stress and tension.

7. Use a small week-at-a-glance calendar and set activities for the next week that will help you achieve your goals. Review it every day and check off your accomplishments

8. If you had one year to live, what would your priorities be?

9. Take time off for yourself in the spaces in the day that you have created by good time management. Don't just take on more responsibilities to fill the gap. Try this little exercise:

   If you have about thirty minutes to spare, find somewhere private you can sit down and relax. Close your eyes and become aware of your breathing. When you feel relaxed enough, think about a beautiful holiday scene. It could be by the mountains, on the beach, in the garden, wherever you like. Create your own holiday video. Absorb the details, see the place, smell the fragrances, hear the birds singing and the waves lapping on the shore. When you have created your little piece of heaven, slowly return to the room and open your eyes. Now you really can get away from it all whenever you like and come back feeling refreshed without anyone knowing you have been away!

10

LOOK AND SOUND LUCKY

Be the kind of irresistible person other people want to help. We all have doubts and fears, and when we meet someone who controls self-doubt and works hard without complaining we instinctively feel at ease and offer them opportunities. A laid-back approach to life gets people on your side.

Keyword: Charm

Charisma is the ability to draw people to you so that they like you and want to help you. Having charisma enhances your chances of being lucky. Charismatic people have something about them that makes it impossible for other people not to be captivated or accommodating.

CHARISMA AND LUCK

Charisma is linked with luck, because both seem to come from divine power. We hope that through our association with charismatic people we can learn their secrets and be like them, in that people will be attracted towards us.

It is assumed that charisma—like luck, hair colour, or height—is something you are born with, but the truth is that we can all work to make ourselves more appealing so that people are more willing to offer us opportunities. Charisma isn't genetic. It can be acquired at any time in your life. Charismatic people do very specific things to make themselves appealing and win the affection of people they meet. Their skills come naturally, but they can also be learned. While you may never have the luminous smile of Julia Roberts or Bill Clinton's twinkle in the eye, you can be more charismatic than you are now.

But take your time. Experts in charisma say it takes about six months to gradually sift new behaviour without confusing the people you already know. 'Charisma is a lot like hair-colour products', says Andrew DuBrin, business professor at Rochester Institute of Technology and a charisma expert. 'You need to introduce changes gradually.' The key is to look at what makes charismatic people tick and to concentrate on learning and practising these qualities until you are comfortable with them. In this chapter you'll learn some of those secrets. Try using the following tricks for natural social success and you'll be right on course to get what you want from other people in all areas of your life: friendship, love, and work.

Carry yourself like a winner

Hold your head high, and lengthen your spine as you walk, letting your breath lift your chest. Feel your head connected to your feet through the straightness of your body, so you're not leading with your head or your stomach. Don't fidget or fiddle with your hands. Send out the message that you feel terrific and you aren't apologising for who or what you are. Be the kind of open person other people would like to get to know.

Always look the part

Dress neatly and colourfully. Do your best to remember names and personal details. Once you get the name-remembering technique under your belt you'll avoid those embarrassing moments of forgetfulness, which can undercut the charismatic impression you want to create. If you make a mistake, don't try to cover it up. Have the courage to admit it and move on.

Act naturally

Tell it like it is, and don't try to be someone you are not.

A FIRM HANDSHAKE

This ranks high among the things that leave a lasting impression. It signifies trust and strength.

SEE EYE TO EYE

Eye contact indicates that you are truly interested in the other person and that you are accessible. You may feel self-conscious at first, but this is a skill that can be learned. Look directly into the eyes of the person you are addressing. When the other person has finished talking, look at his or her eyes and wait a few seconds before you answer. This shows that you are engrossed.

DON'T BE INQUISITIVE

Don't ask people what they do. Instead ask them how they spend their time. Remember, a person is more than his or her job.

CRANK UP YOUR ENERGY LEVELS

Vitality implies youth and courage and hope—the stuff that dreams are made of.

SOUND THE PART

Don't talk too fast. Fast talkers are enthusiastic, but we associate fast talkers with liars, so slow down and take your time.

LAUGH

Laughing makes us feel good, and funny people are more attractive to us.

SMILE

This is one of the best ways to make an impression. A great smile helps you stand out, because it says in the warmest way that you care about the people you meet. It also says that life treats you well, that life is fun and you are lucky. A smile can make a huge difference in the amount of good fortune that comes your way. In a study[29] of adults of various ages, a tendency was found for subjects to mimic the expressions of those around them. In other words, sad faces evoked more sad faces and smiling faces evoked happiness.

Don't get carried away, though. An instant grin carries no weight today. You don't want to be seen as a smiling sycophant. Lucky people don't flash an immediate smile at random. Instead, they look at the other person's face, pause, take in their persona, then smile warmly. The split-second delay shows that the smile is genuine and only for them.

Be interested in other people

The key to charisma is making other people feel special, and the easiest way to do this is to listen and ask questions. Charisma isn't about selling yourself: it is about making other people feel great about themselves. Don't cut off the person talking. You might miss something really important. Unlucky people don't listen; lucky people do.

Be complimentary

Be specific or your praise will sound insincere. Instead of 'nice work' say 'You did X or Y well.' (More on compliments later in this chapter)

Overcome shyness

Charismatic people aren't necessarily the life and soul of the party, but they do know how to overcome shyness. Instead of thinking about yourself when you walk into a room, think about the people in that room. Go and ask how they are feeling, what they are thinking. When you put the attention on other people, shyness will soon disappear.

Wear your heart on your sleeve

You won't be considered charismatic if you are reserved. You have to be excited about what you are talking about. Be positive, and express yourself both verbally and physically. Enthusiastic and open people are appealing. When you show your eagerness, people like to help. We like those who are excited about what they do. It means they are alive and energetic, and helping them makes us feel alive and energetic.

GET LUCKY IN LOVE

The information in this chapter is designed to help you in all aspects of your life—friendship, love, and work—but here are a few tips to help you get lucky in love and stay lucky:

- Make sure you always look your best, whether you are going to work or to the dentist. You never know whom you might meet, and first impressions count.
- If you want to meet someone new you have to get out there to meet them. Find hobbies and interests you enjoy outside the home and commit yourself to a gathering of like-minded people.
- If you want a date you have to make the first move, whether you are a man or a woman. Smile, make eye contact, and see if there is interest. If you are a woman, remember that if you make the first move he will still think it is his idea!
- If you see someone you like, make your presence known fast. Move close enough to talk to him or her, and say something that is neutral and polite. For example, if you are at a wedding you can ask how he or she knows the bride and groom.
- Do your homework. Find out what the person you are interested in likes or dislikes, and put yourself in an advantageous position.
- Be keen, but not too keen.
- Don't make the first date dinner. Research shows that dinner is not the best choice. Plan something that involves a little shared anxiety. You could plan to go for a jog or a walk together, riding, swimming, a play, a film, or a concert. Then if it goes well you can have dinner afterwards to discuss the experience.

- Never forget the magic and artistry of love. Study and practise the techniques of charming people, but when the moment arrives listen to your heart. It will know what to do.

PASSION

You have probably been told all your life not to get carried away or be an open book. If you want to be charismatic, forget that advice. To get that lucky break, you need to let people see how much you want something. Revealing your passion rather than concealing it can be a good-luck strategy. When Madonna wanted the part of Evita she promised she would give it her all. She didn't hold back. She showed the director, Alan Parker, her fire.

When you are passionate you make it clear to people who can help you that this is what you want. When you are passionate it suggests that you will be committed and that you care. By being passionate you encourage others to connect with you personally, and this makes them interested in you. You make them feel they can't say no. And finally, when you are passionate, people long to be around you. Your exuberance is a tonic. When you show your excitement, you give off energy.

You can express your passion in words, but sometimes actions speak louder. You may want to write a letter expressing your desire or to phone the person, even if it is a difficult thing to do. You may have to ask someone you know to make an introduction, even if you feel nervous. You may have to dress up for a meeting, introduce yourself to strangers at a party, do something at very short notice, buy someone a great meal or get on a plane to go after what you want.

WHEN TO TONE IT DOWN

Although enthusiasm is beneficial, coming on too strong or pretending to be enthusiastic when you are not won't work. For enthusiasm to work it needs to be tempting, not restrictive. We all know people who are too pumped up, too optimistic, and the chances are they give us the creeps! Enthusiasm needs to start out low key. If it is used too aggressively or intensely it smacks of desperation. People need to feel motivated, not cornered or embarrassed.

Read your audience for clues about the appropriate level of intensity. If they are squirming, back off and allow for some breathing space. Or if you're speaking to a low-key person you may need to tone it down so they don't get turned off. Be careful not to come on too strong and lose the person you are trying to connect with. Making people laugh can be a great way to relax them.

In some situations passion does not work like a charm. Be reserved with bankers, moneylenders, lawyers, or groups of people who view you as an outsider; too much passion from someone new can make them squirm. Instead, divide and conquer. Meet people individually to win them over. When you are dating don't be too eager with potential partners. Feel your way slowly. Instead of letting someone see how excited you are about meeting a potential partner, let them see your passion for life. For example, if you have a genuine interest in something and are also looking for a potential partner, join a group or club devoted to that interest. Love may come your way, not because you are looking for it but because you are in love with something else.

If you are not a naturally high-energy person you can still be perceived as enthusiastic by showing great interest in the other person. The more pumped up you are about what the other person is telling you, the more you will be thought of as enthusiastic. Ask lots of questions, and don't interrupt. The more interested you are in others, the more enthusiastic you will appear.

Remember, charisma is the art of making people aware that you are paying attention to them. Charisma has nothing to do with egomania. You are feeding other people's desire to be noticed, not holding them captive as you talk about yourself. Putting the spotlight on others makes them feel terrific and, by extension, you. The more special you make other people feel, the more likely they are to do things for you.

I didn't know that

No matter how talented you are, you need something extra to make other people want to go out of their way for you. That something extra is a childlike innocence.

Nobody likes a know-it-all. Demonstrating a sincere openness and willingness to learn will draw people to you, and they will want to help you. Innocence is not the same as ignorance. Innocence is honesty, purity, and simplicity. Ignorance is plain ignorant!

People like to help those who are trying to improve themselves. Why? Because it is rewarding to help someone who is in need of advice and assistance. Don't be ashamed to say you don't know something or you don't understand how something works.

Most people cover the gaps in their knowledge, thinking that to admit them would make them look ignorant and not worthy of opportunity. But you need confidence and courage to let your curiosity show. Asking simple questions means you are confident and self-assured. If you know a little about a lot you are less likely to jump to conclusions, and people are far more willing to help you.

> 'Whenever I am in meetings and I say I don't understand something, at first there is surprise, but then there is relief when it becomes clear that other people in the room haven't a clue what is going on either,' says Martin, who is well on his way to becoming a solicitor. If you are the one asking the simple questions, you often find yourself becoming the one other people are drawn to.

When you ask questions, more things will come to you. Instead of showing how clever you are, it's better to find out how smart others are. If you spend all your energy trying to impress other people, you won't learn much. Let children be your role models. Watch them carefully and try to understand what they do. They can teach you a lot about what matters.

So how do you ask questions in a way that sounds smart, not stupid? 'I must admit that I don't know your world as well as you, but one question I have' is a good place to start. This gets people thinking about how they can help you.

Questions are just a way to begin relationships. Make sure you listen to the answers and don't answer your own questions. Patient listeners know that really important information doesn't come until a minute or two into the answer. If you cut someone off, you might miss something important. Pause for a moment when the other person has finished talking to show that you are taking in what they have said to you.

A great way to assess your ability to listen is to ask if you can tape a conversation with a friend. You will be surprised how often you don't listen properly or are impatient and cut someone off before they have had a chance to answer your question. You don't always have to have an answer or a quick opinion. There is great wisdom in silence. It says, 'I am listening. I am here.'

WHEN PASSION AND INNOCENCE AREN'T ENOUGH

There will be times when you need to take your enthusiasm and curiosity one step further to create luck. Sometimes another person may not be sure what you want. You have to ask for it. Many of us are reluctant to ask for what we want. We feel uncomfortable and fear that we will be humiliated or rejected. But if you ask for something in a polite, respectful and direct way, the other person will usually be impressed, even if he or she isn't prepared to give you what you want.

Be ready to offer people a bonus if they help you out. This sounds obvious, but many of us get so caught up in our own needs and excitement we don't get round to addressing the other person's needs. So reach beyond your own interests when it comes to asking for something; find the other person's personal bonus. Your offer has to be something that they think is valuable and that they would regret passing up.

If you are changing your career you may appear really enthusiastic, but why should someone spend time training and bringing you up to speed? What can you offer them? Perhaps it is maturity, contacts, or setting up a web site. Make sure you make it clear what you have to offer the other person. Find out what they need and what they are looking for. Offer a bonus even if you don't feel the other person deserves it. For example, if you want your husband to take a more active part in child care, let him know how much the children want to see him and how much happier they will be if he spends more quality time with them.

Don't underestimate the power of flowers, muffins, shoulder rubs (for partners you are trying to convince), invitations, meals, freebies. And if you just don't know what their personal bonus is, make sure you make them feel important for saying yes. People love to feel they are part of something that matters. For example, if your children's schoolteacher is not giving your child much attention and you need to convince them to take an interest, say something like, 'You really help shape the future of some of these youngsters. My son is at a critical point in his life right now, and you could play such an important role in sending him in the right direction. If you would help him it would mean the world to us.'

Be nosy

In order to keep moving in the right direction you need a perpetual flow of information and a constant influx of people who can help. The way to do this is not only to be curious but to be nosy. Don't mind your own business!

Lucky people talk to everyone they can; they gather tips, strategies and names that will help them. They keep their eyes and ears open, looking and listening for essential information. Of course you shouldn't do this in a brash, boorish way; otherwise you will end up with nothing.

One of the most effective ways of gathering information is to keep your mouth shut and your eyes and ears open. Observe what is going on and keep your eyes peeled. If you have an important meeting, show up early so you can relax ahead of time or talk to people you might not have a chance to speak to later. Watch how people interact; find out who will be able to help you succeed. And when they help you, remember to show your gratitude.

Time to talk

Keeping your eyes open and your mouth shut works for only so long; eventually you are going to have to talk. You'll get your chance to make your pitch or have your audience with the mentor of your dreams, and it's up to you to present your case in the most persuasive way possible.

Pull out all the stops to look the best you can. People respect you more when you are well dressed. Be open about what you want. Ask for your favour or the help you need first. Make sure you cast the other person in the best possible light. Say, 'You have been terrific to give me so much advice. It will be a big help to me. Is there anything you would suggest I do, any person I should contact?' Accentuate the positives. Throw in a personal bonus. Make things sound better than they are. Ask for their opinion. Get them talking. And, finally, read the signs. Do they seem interested or uncomfortable when you are talking? Time to back off or go full speed ahead?

Be generous with your compliments

Sincere compliments make people feel good. Insincere ones make them feel manipulated. So mind what you say; otherwise you are better off saying nothing. The most powerful compliments are those that praise what isn't obvious. Once your compliment is warmly received, you will likewise be cordially accepted and more likely to receive the help you require.

Saying something complimentary about what the other person has worked hard to perfect will usually go down well. A good word on their work habits or good taste, if sincere, will be well received. Compliments that usually backfire include any mention of a person's weight; how they handled a situation gone bad (no-one wants pity or to be reminded of a tough situation they would like to forget); passing comments on something they did that was mean, such as firing someone or criticising them; praising someone's eyes (sounds great in films but not in real life); complimenting people on things they are afraid of losing, like a 'cute' partner.

Lucky people know how to pay compliments. They know how and when to insist their praise is true and when to drive it home to emphasise their sincerity. When your compliment is sincere and truly touches another person, that person looks with favour on you. The more they feel flattered, the better your chances of attracting more opportunities. People like helping those who make them feel good. They tend to think of these people as special—even lucky.

MAKE IT LOOK EASY

Another thing lucky people do that gets others on their side is not making life look like hard work. Those who make life look easy are universally favoured. Think of great athletes such as Muhammad Ali, admired not just for his brilliant skill but for his ability to float like a butterfly but sting like a bee without showing the strain.

This admiration for people who do tough jobs effortlessly and with good grace extends to our daily lives. We admire the person who always seems to find great jobs without trying hard. We are in awe of the doctor who skilfully manages a back-breaking work load without losing the personal touch for each patient, the lawyer who effortlessly wins a difficult case. We respect people like this because, although we know that what they have done is very difficult and arduous, they don't broadcast the struggle.

I recently heard an interview with Robert Wagner on television promoting his latest film. Wagner, best known for his appearance in the popular love and crime series 'Hart to Hart', has worked steadily from his teens into his seventies. When asked to explain the secret of his success he simply smiled and said with a look of surprise and humility, 'Life has been good to me.' There was no mention of the hours of hard work, dedication, disappointments and sheer drive and determination that got him where he wanted to be.

People who tell us how hard their life is don't make us feel good. We don't want to share their anxiety. We want to believe that you can get what you want without making life a misery. To do well in life you have to be good at what you do and you have to work hard, but to be lucky you need charm. Get angry, frustrated or embarrassed by your limitations and people stop respecting you. Have fun, enjoy yourself and have a great time and people will always come around.

Aren't the best speeches at weddings always delivered by those who are simply enjoying the occasion, not those who are struggling to be witty and clever? Think of your favourite entertainer. Isn't one of the reasons you like them so much the fact that they are so natural and always themselves? Perhaps that is why a flawless performance doesn't move us as much as the entertainer who is simply being himself or herself.

Keep your cool when all around are losing theirs

Lucky people seem to keep their cool when bad luck strikes. They are serious about getting what they want but never seem seriously affected when things go wrong—at least that is the appearance they give. Of course they feel disappointed—they are human after all—but they don't spend long feeling dejected. When you can keep your cool during the tough times, you make life look easy. And when you make life look easy, people assume you are lucky and are more willing to help you.

Why do people who keep their cool under pressure appear lucky? Because we all suffer from low self-esteem to some extent. We sometimes feel that we don't quite fit in or are not quite right for the part. We all question our abilities from time to time, no matter how successful, beautiful or talented we are. That is why we take to people who seem completely at ease with their limitations and who don't let mistakes or failures get them down for long.

When you keep your cool you seem fearless. You allow other people to see your inner strength—your silent power. You inspire others to offer you opportunities. Part of looking and sounding lucky is to control self-doubt and nerves. When you appear nervous you undermine other people's confidence not only in you but in themselves. If you don't appear to be in control, others will pull away from you.

Making what you do look easy will get people on your side. Here are some tips.

- Be prepared. Careful preparation helps you gain control over things that make you feel nervous. The more familiar you are with things, the more you will feel at home. Don't do too much preparation or too little. Do just enough to appear knowledgeable but still open to suggestions.
- Imagine that the people you are interacting with are guests in your sitting-room. They are on your home ground, and therefore you are the one in control.
- If you make a mistake or say something you regret, don't agonise over it; move on quickly. Life isn't perfect, and neither are you. Move on to the next challenge.
- And if you make a mistake, don't try to cover it up. Have the courage to admit it. People can't blame you for making

mistakes; they can blame you for making the same mistake over and over again.

Don't get overconfident

Showing off can lead to bad luck. If you get caught up in your own brilliance you may begin to think your way is the only way. Know-it-alls aren't very lucky, because they are isolated from other people and they appear self-sufficient. Nobody wants to help those who don't need help. Cocky people aren't popular.

Don't take yourself too seriously. According to research, those who spend time having some fun are far more likely to lead a satisfied life.[30] Every time you feel the urge to pontificate or to follow someone's story with your own, ask a question instead and train yourself to listen to the answers. Stop trying to have the last word. And, finally, learn to laugh at yourself. If you take yourself too seriously no-one will think of you as lucky.

One of the best ways to help people relax around you is to be honest about who you are. Don't try to be someone you are not. This takes confidence, but true confidence isn't as difficult as it seems. It is simply the ability to know what your strengths and weaknesses are. Talk to any lucky person and their advice will almost always be, be true to yourself.

If you admit you have the same fears as everyone else, you will get people on your side. When you don't blow your own trumpet you bring people closer to you and make it possible for them to believe that they can do what you did. You inspire them.

Be loyal and true

Being known as a loyal person and friend, who stands by those who help you and knows how to reciprocate a favour when it is due, will stand you in good stead. If you are someone who is willing to go out of your way to help other people, it will show that you are interested in more than your own ego. Don't talk about people behind their back, don't back out of helping others when the request for help is within reason, and be a support to your friends and colleagues when you can.

It can be hard these days to find out the truth. The more powerful people get the more they are surrounded by yes-people who tell them what they want to hear. If you are assertive and not afraid to speak out, you will be admired for your courage. Honesty is risky, as you never know how your comments will be taken or what the reaction will be. But if you are gentle with your honesty and respectful of another person's feelings, you will gain respect from the people that matter.

Do what it takes

In some situations your hard work, enthusiasm, passion and laid-back approach will achieve the desired results, but there are also times when you have to be a little pushy. If you want to be the one chosen you have to be noticed, and noticed for the right reasons. If you have the nerve, here are some strategies that can help you. If you feel uncomfortable about trying them, ignore this section.

Show up

> You don't have to go everywhere, but you do need to show up at places where your presence will remind people that you are in the mix. And don't just show up. Do a Liz Hurley and look amazing. Talk to anyone in a position to change your destiny.

Just in case you didn't see this . . .

> Have a list of people who you know can help you. Make sure you keep in touch with them and let them know how you are progressing. Find out what their interests are, and whenever you come across something relevant, send it to them. People love to be remembered in this way.

SMARTEN UP

Appearance does matter. It is always better to be overdressed with your distinctive style than underdressed. People will give you more respect. Ideas and projects need careful packaging too, so they appear neat, attractive, and in demand.

Neatness is important for luck-making. Look crisp and other people will notice you and feel good about you. When you have taken time about your appearance, you are showing respect for those around you. You are enchanting the environment with colour and order. The purpose of dressing neatly and colourfully isn't to show how stylish you are but to make people feel great when they see you. Colour and co-ordination have a pleasing effect on people psychologically. When you are well groomed and you dress attractively others feel warm towards you, because their senses are stimulated positively.

Do make sure your hair is well groomed, your shoes clean and shiny, your shirt laundered and pressed, and your blouse dry-cleaned. Wear tasteful accessories. Don't dress down, dress younger than your age, or wear loud earrings or ties. And avoid a trendy or retro look. Too much style distracts from the power of your personality.

WANT WHAT YOU HAVE WHILE WORKING FOR WHAT YOU DON'T HAVE

Think hard about what you have achieved so far, and be grateful for it. Luck follows those who appreciate how far they've already come. If you appreciate what you have, your attitude will be much more positive. You won't agonise so much over bad breaks or give up when things don't go your way. Instead, you will see the vivid pattern of your good fortune and concentrate on making more of it come your way. Lucky people realise how fortunate they are.

They feel more upbeat about their lives, and the more upbeat you look and sound, the more people will want to help you get what you want.

Why remind yourself of the things in life you don't have when you could remind yourself of what you do have?[31] People who like what they have are almost twice as happy—and therefore twice as lucky—as those who have more. Lucky people appreciate what they have in life now and in the past. Think of the happy times you, your family and friends have had together, and be grateful for these riches in your life. Contemplating happiness is a powerful way to bring it into the present.

Replace addictions with preferences

Creating luck is about having preferences and doing what it takes to satisfy them without getting attached to them so they become addictions.

Addictions are things we tell ourselves we must have. A preference is something that does not make us miserable if we don't get it. This isn't to say that we are half-hearted about what we want. Happiness involves the maximum effort with the minimum of addiction. Mastering this technique is tough. The next time you think you simply must have something, see if you can turn it into a preference instead: I'd like to have this. I feel more secure when I have this, and so on. Start with small things—like waiting your turn instead of being addicted to pushing ahead—till you progress to the bigger stuff, like not letting a disappointment at work or a disagreement with your partner destroy your self-esteem.

The key is to ask for what you want, not demand it. We teach our children to say please and thank you and to understand that 'no' is often for our own good. It's time to relearn that lesson.

Become a people magnet

To be lucky in life and love you need to have charm. Charming people tend to get whatever they want from anybody, be it business, friendship, or love. Let the information in this chapter help you become a people magnet. Make your people skills your number 1 asset and win hearts wherever you go.

ACTIONS TO TAKE TODAY TO LOOK AND SOUND LUCKY

1. Decide on a goal, and imagine you are reaching it. By vividly imagining this you'll activate the same feeling you would have if you achieved your goal. Picture gain instead of loss, success instead of failure. Hold the feeling of success in your thoughts. Your subconscious mind will supply you with the ideas that will ensure the desired results, and other people will be drawn to your attitude of positive expectancy.

2. The next time you catch yourself complaining, stop and take a deep breath. Ask yourself, is it really necessary for me to burden other people with my worries right now? Do you really need to be the one who never has time for socialising or fun? If your work load is too heavy, ask for help or delegate some of your responsibilities to colleagues or family members.

3. Draw the line between being cocky and being lucky. Nobody wants to help someone who doesn't seem to need help. Make life look easy, but don't rub it in. Make other people feel great about themselves by asking how they feel or praising them sincerely.

4. What are you willing to do, even if you are not in the mood, to bring you good things in your life? Be honest about your laziness or unwillingness to do what it takes. Think about the things you want but for which you aren't willing to make the effort.

5. Imagine that tomorrow you will wake up and everything you

have now is gone: your health, your family, your job—everything. Wouldn't you long to have it all back? Remember that you have all those things now.

6. Imagine you are ninety years old. Looking back, what do you appreciate about your life now? What would you wish you had taken advantage of? If you have children, think about the joy they bring, not the stress. When you are old and grey you will wish you could see them more.

7. Read inspirational stories of people who overcame the odds and achieved what they wanted. Read spiritual books that remind you of this principle.

8. Think about your friends. Who makes your life easy? Who doesn't? Make a serious effort to seek out those who think positively, and limit the time you spend with the ones who see themselves as victims or who drag you down.

9. The next time you are introduced to someone new, make a real effort to remember their name and a few personal details.

11

Don't Have Enemies

All it takes is one careless act that hurts someone's feelings to ruin your reputation. Your reputation is the key to your luck; but your reputation is worthless if nobody trusts or likes you. Lucky people view everyone they meet as potential lifelines. Don't make an enemy of anyone—especially yourself. Learn to let others—and yourself—off the hook.

Keyword: Humility

We have all heard those horror stories about how the smallest things can prevent people from getting the opportunities they deserve: unpleasant comments that were not forgotten; disagreements and misunderstandings that fester; careless acts that hurt other people's feelings. The way people think about you is the key to your luck. If you have enemies, you invite bad luck in. And the worst part of all this is that you may not even be aware of how badly you have hurt your chances of success until it is too late. It's impossible to control other people's reactions to you, but it is possible to play your part in preventing hard feelings between people.

Lucky people regard everyone they meet as potential luck-makers. You never know who could eventually be of help. Little things do matter. There should always be time for politeness, helpfulness, sensitivity, decency, and caring.

There is no excuse for lack of manners or decency. Oversights and mistakes can come back to haunt you. Thankfully, if you have hurt someone's feelings there are often opportunities to heal that situation. You can do much to undo the damage and improve your chances of luck by finding out how the other person felt and apologising sincerely.

Don't burn your bridges

One of the most effective ways to avoid bad luck is to have as few enemies as possible. Here are some tips to help fireproof your bridges.

- Don't harshly criticise family and friends. Critical words from loved ones cut deeply. Even if you are right you create bad feeling in these most important relationships. Studies[32] show that criticism within relationships reduces happiness significantly. Try to remember how much more important these people are to you than the issue you are discussing. Love your family and friends for who they are, and if you must say something critical, always be constructive. Make your criticism reflect your love and respect and not your disappointment.

- Treat important people as if they are important—even if you don't work for them or think of them as important. People like that often have influence over others who can help you.

- Treat less important people as if they are important too. Don't play favourites to the rich and famous and ignore others. You never know who holds the key to good fortune. Someone who appears to be less influential may nevertheless know exactly the right person for you, and this one contact could change your life.

- Never forget to thank someone for a favour, a gift, a promotion, or an opportunity. There is nothing more powerful when it comes to creating a good reputation than a sincere and gracious note or gift of thanks.

- Be sensitive about how you are coming across to others. If you have upset someone, their demeanour will shift for a few seconds before they put up their mask. Look for expressions of surprise or a change of tone that shows they have been taken off their guard. Tiny things—the tone of voice, body language, facial expression, the words used—can communicate volumes. Research suggests that only 7 per cent of meaning is carried in the words you choose; 55 per cent is carried in your body language and the tone of your voice. People[33] who display sensitivity in communication and recognise subtle changes in demeanour are often more satisfied with their relationships than those who do not.

- If you get a chance, never hesitate to do favours for people—even if that favour isn't immediately returned. You never know when you might need that person's help. If someone smart or important lets you down, don't show your disappointment or anger. Far better to be a friend they can't remember than an enemy they can't forget.

- Be a peacemaker. If family and friends are upset with each other, you will feel their unhappiness. Try to be the voice of reason and reconciliation.

- Face your difficulties. To maintain happiness within relationships, research[34] shows that problems must be faced rather than avoided. For the sake of being agreeable some people try to avoid tension. But it is important to raise the subject of disagreement in a loving and constructive way. Freedom of communication in relationships increases the chances of happiness significantly.[35]

- Apologise. Saying sorry when you overreact or make a stupid mistake can quickly turn things around for you. But it takes courage to apologise. Don't let your ego get in the way of admitting you were wrong. Apologies disarm people. When people are offended they tend to go on the offensive; when you apologise you take away their desire to fight you.

- Always apologise in person or on the phone if you have upset someone. This is more personal than a written note, and it also avoids preserving your mistake in writing. Allow your mistakes to be forgiven and forgotten by having the courage to face the person you have wronged and making peace with them face to face.

- Build trust through sending clear and consistent messages to others. You know how hurtful it can be when you like someone and they haven't the courage to let you know that the friendship isn't going to go any further. Whenever you get into a new job or relationship, be clear in your communications so that others don't have the chance to build mistaken assumptions.

- Do what you say you are going to do. Research[36] has shown that commitment to following through on agreed changes makes all the difference between a happy and an unhappy relationship. Nothing destroys progress or enthusiasm more than someone who promises but never follows through. It is crucial that you stay focused and committed to what you say you will do. Credibility is like the bottom of a ship. If it has holes it doesn't matter whether it is big or little: the ship will still sink. If you find you can't keep a commitment, for whatever reason, let the other person know why. If people don't trust you, opportunities won't come your way.

- Stay loyal. Gossip and rumours have destroyed more reputations and relationships than all other bad habits combined. Lucky people are loyal. They keep secrets. They don't break their confidence. Always avoid gossip. This doesn't mean you can't talk about people, but do so in a constructive way. Avoiding gossip takes courage, but people will admire you for it.

- Take courage from your happy relationships, but don't expect each one to be perfect. Don't let tension with one person convince you that you lack the ability to get along with others. It is normal to get along with most but not all of our loved ones. Research[37] has shown that the most satisfied people do not have happy relationships with everyone. They appreciate their happy ones and accept that some aren't going to be perfect. They create happiness from the relationships they have and do not need all their relationships to fit an ideal image.

- Keep in touch. Try not to cut yourself off from your roots. Think about and celebrate your national identity. Often we feel lost in a complex world. Studies[38] show there is comfort in knowing your racial and national heritage.

- Keep your family close if you can. Studies[39] have shown that family relationships are an important indicator of happiness for adults of all ages. As family members scatter across the world it becomes easy to forget to include them in your life. Keep in contact and share your news. You will feel better if loving bonds are maintained.

- And, most important of all, learn to listen. Listening can build bridges. Not listening can tear them right down. The key to conflict-free relationships is to listen first, and talk second.

Everyone wants to be understood, and the key to understanding is listening. Poor listening styles include pretending to listen, not paying attention to facial or body language, listening to what we want to hear, seeing things only from our own point of view, judging, giving advice when it hasn't been asked for, and interrogating, asking lots of questions when people aren't prepared to open up.

To genuinely listen you need to do four things:

1. Pay attention to what people are saying. Listen for tone, and watch body language.
2. Put yourself in the other person's shoes. Try to see the world as they see it and feel as they feel it. Conversations are not competitions. It is silly to try to win them.
3. Think like a mirror. A mirror doesn't judge or give advice. It reflects. When someone really needs to be heard, try mirroring their words back to them. Mirroring phrases you can use to practise include: 'As I understand it you feel that,' 'So, as I see it,' 'I can see that you are feeling,' 'So what you are saying is.'
4. Give constructive feedback. Ask yourself, 'Will this feedback help the person, or am I just doing it to suit myself?' Send 'I' messages, not 'you' messages. Say, 'I'm concerned that you aren't doing well,' not 'You aren't doing well.' People feel threatened if you are passing judgment.

Revenge isn't sweet

Revenge isn't sweet: it's stupid. Some people sever their links with key contacts by reacting out of anger in a way that alienates people. The trouble is they sacrifice long-term benefits for the short-term satisfaction of getting even.

When Harry's colleague was promoted and he wasn't, Harry was furious. He had worked in the same company for fifteen years, and this was outrageous. He decided to go freelance and gave just four weeks' notice. He was asked if he could stay a few more weeks to ease in a new member of staff, but he refused, saying that the company had let him down, so why should he help them.

Unfortunately for Harry, many of the people he let down at that time left the company and took their memories of him with them. Even though they understood why Harry did what he did, they had formed an opinion of him that he was reckless and disloyal. Had he departed with a little more grace he might have been held in higher regard. As it was, Harry burned his bridges. His freelance career never took off, and he is now working in another company several rungs down the ladder.

Carrying around grudges leads to stress, anger, and eventually bad luck. People don't like to help those who are bitter or motivated by anger. As soon as your grudge becomes public you will have poisoned your well. Forcing yourself to drop grudges will free you to think positively and concentrate on what is important. So sidestep or ignore people who hurt you. Imagine that they are helping you become stronger and more resourceful instead. Never talk openly about people you dislike—your image will suffer; and if you must gossip, cast that person in a positive light. When you bury your grudges you become more upbeat and people will want to be around you and help you.

If you can find it within yourself to act graciously and not erupt with anger when things don't go according to plan, you will win respect. The more you take difficulties in your stride and demonstrate your resilience, the more likely it is that others will offer you opportunities in the future. Resist the temptation to get your own back—even when the people who let you down are down themselves. You are better off helping them up. No-one respects people who kick the underdog. And finally, don't forget that disappointments are only temporary. Don't waste time dwelling on them; get right back to work making a new plan.

Control your temper

No-one thinks clearly when their fists are clenched. Disappointment often leads to anger. Letting off steam may feel good, but it also creates bad luck. The better you are able to control yourself, the more you will be respected and the less likely you are to have enemies. Hot-tempered people have no allies; they don't get the best out of other people, and it almost always backfires.

The idea that letting yourself go makes you feel better has taken deep root. But, as Daniel Goldman showed in his book *Emotional Intelligence*, psychologists' tests in recent decades have repeatedly shown that giving vent to anger does little or nothing to dispel it, although it might feel momentarily satisfying. The trouble is anger clouds your thinking process, and if you let anger get the better of you, you are less likely to think about what you want and are thus less likely to get it. If you want to keep your cool when all around are losing theirs, you need to learn two vital skills: how to approach arguments strategically, and how to behave more assertively to prevent yourself exploding in anger when you get into situations where you feel cornered.

Four strategies for resolving arguments

1. Be a good listener. Listening is crucial to winning arguments, as it makes the other person feel they have had their say. Once they have done this, they might be more prepared to come around to your point of view. Allow the other person to finish speaking before you speak.
2. Pause for thought. To resolve an argument in your favour you need to calm the person you are talking to. Acknowledge the speaker's feeling and allow a pause in the conversation to allow both of you to consider what has been said. Use the word 'we' to explore possible solutions, thus avoiding apportioning blame. Suggest how you might work together in the future.

3. Count to ten. Many arguments stem from misunderstandings. Wait ten minutes before replying to an enraging e-mail, and delay at least one day before answering a letter. If you are in a face-to-face conversation be aware of your body language so you are sending a consistent message.
4. Allow some space. Give the other person room to change his or her position without losing face. This is one of the most important rules of negotiation. Make sure the other party can walk away from any agreement you might reach with something to show for it—even if the argument has gone in your favour.

Seven steps to assertive behaviour

1. Be prepared to take risks; this is essential to assertive behaviour.
2. Stop blaming other people for how you feel and accept that you are angry because you choose to be. Resolve to use your anger to find a resolution to the problem.
3. Learn to say no. Try, 'Let me think about it' or 'I can't do it today but perhaps I can tomorrow.' Then stop talking. Silence is a powerful tool.
4. Use your voice as a weapon. The lower it is, the more powerful the effect. Don't raise your voice at the end of a sentence. It sounds less credible.
5. Use assertive language: 'I have a question,' not 'Can I ask a question?' 'Let me interrupt' instead of 'May I interrupt?' and 'I'm good at' instead of 'I'm not bad at.'
6. Reward yourself. Changing behaviour is difficult, so congratulate yourself each time you direct your anger in a positive way.
7. It takes twenty-one days to establish a habit. So if you can keep up your assertive behaviour for three weeks without slipping, it should start to become second nature.

Teach others how to treat you

> You are being assertive when you stand up for yourself. You communicate your needs clearly and respect the rights and feelings of other people. We teach people the way we want them to treat us. This means that if people aren't treating you well, it is because you have let them do so. If you don't feel good about yourself the chances are you are letting someone treat you badly. Change this relationship by changing your behaviour. Act assertively and people who aren't treating you well will either change their behaviour or leave your life.

Certainly there is a time and place for expressing outrage. If you see cruelty or someone trying to take advantage, outrage will get people's attention. There are also times when you simply lose your cool. It is only when anger becomes the norm that it becomes dangerous to your luck. The secret is not to deny anger but to get angry in a positive way. You can show you are angry, but without losing control. Don't take it personally; ask questions to put distance between you or simply walk away. In short, you know yourself well enough to get out of a situation before it explodes.

When life goes your way

Don't brag when life goes your way. People will either resent you or wish you bad luck. Good fortune and bad fortune alike visit all of us, so why would you want to feel superior? Master the art of quiet contentedness and you'll get a lot further. True happiness is inner peace, self-satisfaction, and fulfilment. If you share your feelings of happiness, do so in a way that respects the feelings of others. Modesty and privacy are the best protections between you and bad luck. Share good news with your friends and bad news with your enemies.

Despite your best efforts, there will always be those who want to cut you down to size. Bear in mind that people who are envious simply want you to pay attention to them. Share a little of your good fortune. If this doesn't work, stay away from them entirely. Try to think less about the people and things that bother you. Remember, those who regularly ruminate over negative feelings and unhappiness are 70 per cent less likely to feel happy than those who do not.[41] Don't make yourself part of their world and they will soon lose interest. The less you interact with them, the less likely it is that they will create bad luck for you.

The power of forgiveness

However well you control your anger, there is no denying that when someone does something to you that upsets you or causes problems, you will feel angry, disappointed, and betrayed. Disappointment is a fact of life.

> Suppose a friend promised to baby-sit so you could go to see your favourite singer in concert but at the last moment lets you down for not a very convincing reason and you can't go. The next day she apologises, but you are still fuming. You find it hard to forgive her: she knew how much you were looking forward to the concert. She offers to make it up to you and take you out to lunch. You don't understand why she couldn't have done this one thing for you. You go to lunch and make small talk, but you are still angry.
>
> When you arrive at the restaurant the menu is delicious, but you can't enjoy yourself. The food tastes bitter and you feel very tired. You want to enjoy the occasion but you can't.

Holding a grudge may feel like you are teaching another person a lesson, but what it is really doing is shutting down your positive energy and pushing luck away. Feeling angry will also make you feel ill and tired.

It really is true that holding a grudge will hurt only one person—you. Forgiveness is tough. It's a bit like regular exercise: it's hard to do it, but you know it will make you feel better. When you are filled with anger you can move forward in life, but the part of you available for luck is not being used.

Give them a break

Richard Carlson became a best-selling author writing about how pointless it is to 'sweat the small stuff.' Don't ignore what bothers you, but don't concentrate on it to the exclusion of the things you enjoy.

If you look hard enough, there is something about everybody that could annoy you. But when you are indignant about other people's behaviour, ask yourself if this is how you would want to be treated for *your* imperfections. Are your own weaknesses any worse than theirs? Is this really such a big deal?

If you are going mad because the telephone operator is having problems transferring you to the correct line, you have a choice: you can get angry and tell her she is incompetent, or you can imagine how she must feel trying to master a new job, dealing with impatient customers all day, feeling inadequate in handling such an apparently simple job. Or perhaps she has personal problems or a learning difficulty or can't concentrate today because her dog was run over last night. We all have days like that. Give her a break!

Whenever people annoy you, take a look at yourself and why you want to change them. Give them the benefit of the doubt. Rather than assuming that hurtful behaviour was intentional, why not assume that they were unskilled, overwhelmed, careless and imperfect—just as you are sometimes? They may have had good intentions but the results were not positive. Whenever you get angry with someone's weaknesses, try looking for their strengths. You will find it easier to feel compassion.

> Whenever you feel yourself getting upset or annoyed about something trivial, ask yourself this question: 'Does it really matter?' If it does, be sure to talk about it to the right person.

However, you may find yourself getting worked up about something that is really unimportant. Is it worth getting upset that the house isn't completely tidy? Is it worth getting upset because someone at work used your mug? When you are feeling good about yourself these minor irritations are unimportant. It's only when we are feeling low that they seem to matter. The next time you become annoyed with minor details, ask yourself, 'Does it really matter?' If the answer is no, then tell yourself it does not matter, let go, and move on.

STAY AWAY FROM BLAME

It's easy to blame other people when things don't go the way we want. I would have done so well if so-and-so hadn't done this or that, and so on. It may be true that other people did things that don't help you, but holding yourself back because of them will harm only you.

Blame makes you feel powerless about being able to bring luck into your life. You can't change the past, but you can change the future. People are not unlucky just because circumstances have gone against them. They continue to create bad luck through blame and lack of forgiveness and therefore lose opportunities that could turn around their fate.

Take responsibility for your problems or setbacks and try not to lay the blame on other people. Otherwise it sounds as if you are making excuses, which is the language of losers. Excuses are self-defeating, and once you start to make them you neglect to take steps to improve your performance. The secret is to learn from your mistakes and do things differently the next time. Don't fall into the blaming trap. It's a hard habit to kick.

LET YOURSELF OFF THE HOOK

And don't forget to stop blaming the most significant person in your life: you. Beating yourself up will make you feel depressed and hopeless and ultimately damage your chances of luck. Depression leads to inaction, which stops good things happening to you.

In many ways the drive to improve is a healthy thing. People who set themselves realistic goals are sane and well-adjusted perfectionists. However, high expectations cause a problem if they lead to a fear of making mistakes or if they leave you feeling like a failure if things don't go according to plan.

Give yourself a break! Let's say you made a big mistake or did something really stupid. It could be a little thing: you put coloured clothes in with a white wash and everything came out pink, you locked yourself out of the house, or you forgot your passport. Or it could be something bigger. Your boss caught you making personal calls at work, you overspent your budget, lost on the stock market, had an affair, or said things you regret. Immediately you start to accuse yourself. How could you be so stupid? This isn't going to get you anywhere. Self-castigation won't achieve anything. So what should you do?

Imagine that you are four years old. Speak to yourself gently, as you would if you were a toddler. Gentle self-talk is far more productive than berating yourself. Instead of using negative words such as 'I'm so stupid' say 'Maybe I could try something different the next time.' Take a deep breath and calm down. This will slow you down and make the problem seem more manageable. If you can, step outside yourself and have a laugh. Look at things in perspective, and watch the way you speak to yourself.

Turn regret into resolve

When you make mistakes it is important to learn from them and to hold yourself accountable. Regret can be very useful for a short time; otherwise you would keep repeating the same mistakes and messing up your life. But after you have felt regret, make amends and do all you can to set it right. It is time to move on and make luck. The potential for creating luck for yourself and others is strongest when you feel compelled by a need to set right what was wrong. So use that energy. Turn regret into resolve to make a positive difference right now.

Even though you wish the mistake had never happened, make it the best thing that ever happened. Find other people to help you. Work hard at loving and appreciating people you have hurt. Get professional counselling if you need to. Do what you can to avoid making the same mistake again. Let go of the past, and be a living example to others of how to create good from bad.

YOU CAN'T PLEASE EVERYONE

One of the quickest ways to chase luck right out of your life is to make other people's approval your first priority. If you want to make everyone admire you, you may end up saying yes when you should say no. Women often feel guilty for saying no or letting other people down. This drive to be loved by everyone leads them to take actions that are not in their own or others' best interests.

SAY YES TO LUCK

It helps, when you need to say no, to think you are saying yes to yourself. This may sound selfish, but it isn't. When you say no you allow someone else to say yes. That person who needs help may find someone else who can provide it better than you can. Saying no isn't easy if paid work or a loved one's feelings are involved, but if you are stretched too thin you have to imagine that another person can benefit from that same opportunity as much as you can. Don't be the person blocking another person's luck. Offer opportunities you can't cope with to others. If you are worried about hurting your partner's feelings because you can't make a commitment, think about how your 'no' will free them for the right man or woman, who will really love and appreciate them the way they deserve. Hanging on to a relationship because you don't want to hurt someone may prevent them from meeting a sensational person who could make them very happy.

Sometimes well-meaning attempts to protect others from pain has the opposite effect: it hurts them even more. Saying no to others and yes to yourself allows you to concentrate on what you really need. It allows you to help the people you are meant to help instead of the ones your need for approval drives you to serve. Saying yes to what you really want will almost certainly mean you have to say no to other things or people. When you can do that, you open the doors to luck, and you won't be one of those unlucky souls lying on their deathbed saying, 'I wish I had . . .'

Think win-win

Life isn't about competition or getting ahead, yet many of us act as if it were. We may think the pie of success is only so big, that if someone gets a big slice there is less for me. This is a win-lose attitude, which increases your chances of having enemies. If you adopt a win-lose attitude you are using other people for your own gains, trying to get ahead at the expense of other people, always insisting on getting your way without concerning yourself about the feelings of others and becoming jealous when something good happens to other people. In the end, win-lose usually backfires. You could end up the winner, but you won't be a very happy one and you won't have many friends.

Others fall into the trap of lose-win. Lose-win looks prettier, but it is just as dangerous. It's the doormat approach to life. Do what you like to me. Wipe your feet on me. Everybody else does. Lose-win is weak. It is easy to get stepped on; it is easy to be the nice guy, it is easy to give in, all in the name of peace. It is easy to set low expectations and to compromise. It is easy to hide your true feelings. For little issues, like who gets what mug at the office, lose-win is fine. But on the important things, you must take a stand. If you don't, no-one will respect you, and you certainly won't find happiness or fulfilment.

A lose-lose approach to life says, 'If I'm going down, you are coming down with me.' Misery loves company. War is a good example of lose-lose. Whoever kills most people in the war wins. Is this really winning?

Now let's turn our attention to win-win, the only approach to life that gets other people on your side and minimises the risk of disagreements. Win-win is a belief that everyone can win. It's being strong and accommodating at the same time. You care about other people and want them to do well, but you also care about yourself and you want to succeed too. Win-win is abundant. You believe there is enough success to go around. It's not you or me: it's both of us. It's not a matter of who gets the biggest slice: there is enough for everyone.

It sounds simple, but it isn't so easy in real life. How do you do it? How can you be happy for a friend who just got a great job when you didn't? How do you find solutions to problems that help everyone? It all begins with you. If you are insecure and emotionally dependent on other people, it will be difficult to think win-win. Building your self-esteem, which we discussed earlier, is the foundation for thinking win-win. The next step is to stop competing and comparing.

Competition is healthy only when it drives you to improve and become your best. Competition is unhealthy when you tie your self-worth to winning or when you use it as a way to impress others. Use competition as a benchmark for measuring yourself, but stop competing over relationships, status, popularity, positions, attention, and the like.

Comparing yourself to others is sure to undermine your luck. Every person has their own path in life, with its own obstacles. It does no good at all to switch to someone else's path to see how they are doing. You feel vulnerable, like a reed blown in the wind, feeling inferior one minute and superior the next, confident one moment and intimidated the next. Research[41] shows that making comparisons with other people reduces happiness significantly. The best way is to compare yourself with your own potential.

Win-win brings luck

Win-win is a luck-maker. If you are committed to helping others to succeed and willing to share recognition you will become a magnet for friends. Think about it: don't you just love people who want you to win? It makes you want to help them in return? Think about how good it feels when everyone gets a piece of the cake. What a miserable birthday it would be if you ate all your cake and didn't give anyone a slice!

Sometimes, however hard you try, it seems impossible to create a win-win situation. Say, for example, your partner wants to get engaged and you don't. When this happens you can try to find a solution, but failing that, it might be time to quit and go your separate ways. There is no point in dwelling on unwinnable conflicts. The problems you spend your time and energy on should be both important and improvable. Otherwise you are better off moving on to things you can change.

You'll know when you have a win-win approach to life because of the way you are feeling. With the other approaches your judgment will feel clouded and you will be plagued by negative feelings. But win-win will make you feel happy and secure. You will act in the best interests of everyone—including you. You will be making friends, not enemies—and friends are the best guarantees of good luck.

Actions to take today to let yourself and others off the hook

1. List two mistakes or disappointments in your life. Then think about how these experiences led you to something positive in your life or in someone else's. How did you make luck out of something bad?

2. Think of one mistake in your life that you regret. Then think how you have *not* made something positive come out of it. How did you stop yourself moving forward? What do you

need to do to make amends and turn this unfortunate incident into luck?

3. Ask yourself who you need to forgive so that you can move on with your life. What is stopping you, and what can you do today to move you closer to letting go and moving forward?

4. Without caring if you win or lose, play a game with others for the fun of it, for example Monopoly or chess. If you prefer outdoor activities, how about a friendly game of squash, golf, or football?

5. The next time someone close to you succeeds, feel happy for them, not threatened. Send them a congratulatory card or a bunch of flowers. Go up to them, shake their hand, and say, 'Well done!'

6. Think about your attitude to life. Is it based on win-lose, lose-win, lose-lose, or win-win? How is that attitude affecting you?

7. Pick one important relationship that is damaged. It may be with a parent, a sibling, or a friend. Now commit yourself to rebuilding that relationship one step at a time. The other person may wonder what you are up to, but stick with it. It could take months to build, but little by little they will see that you are genuine and really want to make things work.

8. Spend a morning listening. Talk only when you have to.

9. Ask yourself what your listening style is. What do you have the biggest problem with? Are you too quick to give advice? Are you listening selectively? Now try to go through the afternoon and evening without doing that.

12

Balance Giving and Receiving

Lucky people tend to be very generous people: generous with their time, money, ideas, or resources. When you help other people without expecting or asking for repayment, you double your chances of good luck, not just because they might help you in return one day but because the joy created by your generosity will make you feel good about yourself. And when you feel good about yourself you feel more optimistic, which automatically makes you someone other people want to help.

Keyword: Generosity

Giving and receiving is what making luck is essentially about. When you help someone without expecting anything in return, you double your chances of luck. First of all, the happiness you feel when you are generous will make you feel good about yourself. You feel optimistic and upbeat and are more likely to attract luck with a positive frame of mind. Secondly, the people you have helped may one day help you. Generosity is contagious. And, finally, if you are generous other people assume you must be lucky and are more likely to offer you opportunities, as you appear to have no doubts that you can easily replace what you have given away.

An Aesop fable

> Two men were travelling together on a road. One of them found a purse of money someone had lost on the way. 'Look what I have found!' he cried. 'It is very heavy. It must be full of money.' And indeed the purse was full of gold coins. 'You should say how lucky *we* are,' his companion said. 'Aren't we travelling together? Companions should share everything.' 'No,' replied the other man. 'I found it, and I am going to keep it.'
>
> A little later they were stopped by a mob of angry people shouting, 'Stop thief!' The man who had picked up the purse went pale with fright. 'We are lost if they find the purse on us,' he cried. 'They will think we stole it.' But his companion was not frightened. 'Don't say *we* are lost,' he said. 'You would not say *we* before, so why say it now?'

Moral: If you do not share your success, do not expect others to share in your disappointments.

The luck exchange

When you help someone else you have no idea how your actions will eventually translate into luck for yourself. It's a bit like throwing a pebble into a river: your energy ripples out, touching many lives. You may not know where your luck comes from until it happens. The trick of luck-making is that you have to help others without knowing if luck will come back to you. You trust that if you are kind and helpful, luck will return to you like a boomerang.

Let's say you take the time to advise a student who wants to work in the same field as you. While you are chatting the student learns that you enjoy music, as you often mention famous composers when you are speaking. You don't see the student again. But six months later she sends you advance information about a series of concerts taking place at her university. You decide to attend. When you arrive you bump into an old friend you haven't seen for years. You swap phone numbers and agree to have dinner at her house. You go to dinner, and there you are reacquainted with someone who shares your passion for music, and it progresses from there. You fall in love and get married.

Lucky people give unconditionally. The more they give, the luckier they become, because their efforts are selfless and without condition, which makes people want to repay them. Others may recommend you for an opportunity or may work hard to repay you or go out of their way to give you suggestions and advice. Generosity breeds loyalty and guarantees you a place in people's minds, and that is often all you need to improve your luck.

Sometimes the good feeling that comes from the act of giving makes you feel so worth while that you undergo a transformation and are attracted to new circumstances that bring good luck into your life. Generosity's true reward isn't a favour returned but the warmth you feel after you have given. You feel good about yourself, and your image and reputation are enhanced. Research has proved that regular volunteer work increases life expectancy, decreases boredom, and creates an increased purpose in life. Volunteer workers are twice as likely to feel happy as non-volunteers.[42]

If you want to lift yourself up, the best way is often to lift others up. But shouldn't you give without wanting anything in return? Let's face it: most of us give not just because we want to help but because it makes us feel good. There isn't anything wrong with that. It's the way the world works.

It is almost impossible to give with no strings attached; but if you expect repayment you are setting yourself up for disappointment and you are limiting your luck. Your attitude becomes sour and you become bitter and resentful. These negative emotions tarnish your lucky image. Giving has to be motivated by the true spirit of generosity. You give and then forget about it.

No luck-making strategy should have as its aim manipulation and deception. Give from your heart, not your head, and never give under false pretences in order to manipulate someone. Don't give when it is likely to cause you resentment, and never approach giving like a bookkeeper. The credit for your compassion may not show up for a long time, and it may never show up at all, except in your heart. Give without asking, and sometimes give without anyone else knowing. And, finally, give when you need to be reminded of how lucky you already are.

DO SMALL THINGS WITH GREAT LOVE

Have you ever felt that everything is going wrong, and then suddenly someone does something nice to you and turns your day around? Sometimes the smallest things—a hello, a kind note, a smile, a compliment, a hug—can make a huge difference. In relationships the little things are often the big things. Add small acts of kindness and see your luck improve. Here are some suggestions. Try adding other ideas of your own.

* Offer someone a compliment.
* Call in on an elderly neighbour for five minutes a day to make sure they are all right.
* Drop off some flowers to a nursing-home with a request that it be given to someone who doesn't get many visitors.
* Let the person behind you in the supermarket with only a few items go ahead of you.
* At a restaurant, pile up your dishes neatly to make it easier for the waiter to clear.
* Call your mother or father to say hello.
* Let a driver into the traffic.
* Offer to baby-sit for a couple who can't get out much.

Giving help is a win-win situation, so pay attention to your surroundings and offer help if you can. It could be as simple as holding the door open for the person behind you. It's a gesture of friendliness that makes a person feel better and makes you feel good about yourself.

In experimental research[43] into the relationship between happiness and helping behaviour, life satisfaction has been shown to improve significantly with the level of altruistic activity. By helping others we create positive bonds with others and enhance our self-image. Those who had more opportunities to help felt much better about themselves than those who didn't have so many opportunities. Take the time to help, comfort or just be with those you care about when they are in need. Studies[44] show that difficult circumstances in a person's life are a less strong predictor of their happiness or unhappiness than the amount of support available to them.

Follow the golden rule and treat others as you would want them to treat you. Think about what an offer of help means to someone else, not to you. If you ever have something nice to say, just say it. Don't wait until people are dead to send flowers. Tell other people how much you care. If you are concerned about feeling vulnerable, stop viewing relationships as a competition and more of a celebration. You don't win at relationships. You win by having relationships.

Think about what motivates you to give and what stops you giving. Think about what kind of giving activities give you most satisfaction and what kind make you feel burned out and resentful. Then think about what you would like to do to increase the giving behaviour that makes you feel good. Look for ways to do random acts of kindness daily. Try it for a week and notice how giving behaviour not only makes you feel great but brings you luck.

Go out of your way

Give when people are down on their luck. This is the best time to offer help. That's when most people desert them and when they need most support. They won't ever forget your help and will always be grateful, because you helped them when they really needed it. They also know that they might not have had the courage to do what you did if you had been in the same situation. It takes a lot of strength to help someone who is down. But once they are up on their feet you have a friend for life.

Follow up with additional help. Most people won't ask you for additional assistance once you have helped them. That's why a follow-up phone call to see how they are doing is so greatly appreciated, even if your help doesn't produce results.

If you can't give help, give hope, friendship, or a confidence boost. This doesn't cost you anything but is highly appreciated. Go that extra mile. Don't hold back. You may find that it is the best thing you have ever done.

Share the spotlight

It is human nature to want to be thought of as sole owner or creator, but denying other people a piece of the pie can be foolish. It limits your luck, because it shuts people out, people who may be able to help you one day. Lucky people give credit, share their success, and win opportunities.

Recognition has a powerful long-term payoff. When you recognise someone for the help they have given you, they will steer opportunities your way. Giving credit requires not only generosity but courage and honesty, and when you give it you will be respected. It shows that you don't care about your ego: you care about the project, the idea, the goal, the relationship. Recognise other people and they will feel valued.

People who are lucky can afford to give other people credit because they are secure and in touch with their inner strength. They don't get defensive and protective about their ideas, because they know that if they do, others become less willing to help or get involved. If you insist on being a self-sufficient hero, people may fear you and work against you. When you give others a chance to participate and reward them for their efforts, they respect and admire you. So give other people credit when they deserve it, share your ideas, and praise other people's efforts. Not only will you make friends for life but your luck will improve.

Seeking advice from important people

Lucky people who are great at setting aside their egos and sharing credit have a good eye for those with resources. They pinpoint smart, hard-working people who can improve their luck; they seek their advice and they give them credit. The lucky also know that important people are more likely to help you if they have a stake in your achievement. Listen to their advice, keep them informed if you follow up their leads, and show how their help changed you, your work, or your good fortune. It is one thing to ask for help and quite another to show how you benefited from that help. Such a move is confirmation that you take their advice and wisdom seriously.

> Shelly was an artist keen to get her works exhibited. She realised that she was not going to be in the big league of genius whose work is always exhibited. She also knew that there were hundreds of artists like her whose work was very good, but that the only way she would get noticed was to get others to promote her. She met a curator who gave her some suggestions about how she could change the direction of her work. Rather than let her ego rule, she valued the comments of an expert and made some changes. When she had her next show she sent him an invitation, with a note saying how his advice had helped. Later that week he called to say that he had recommended that his gallery acquire one of her works. By allowing the curator to become part of her work she was able to make good luck happen in a way that many artists can only dream about.

Keep important people informed of your progress if they have helped. When you ask for help you have in effect sold a piece of yourself. You owe your investors regular updates. Sometimes something as simple as a thank-you or an update can make or break your luck. When you thank people, you allow them to feel good about helping you.

Don't get greedy and expect a few important contacts to make things happen for you every time. Pinning your hopes on one person to make your dreams come true puts too much pressure on them. Always assume that people would like to do their best to help you, but don't expect it, or you set yourself up for disappointment. Be at ease, don't pile the pressure on, and remain open and optimistic. It's amazing how good you feel when you are nurturing, sharing, and giving, no matter what happens.

And remember to share a little of yourself too. Research[45] has shown that people who tend to be socially open rate their overall life satisfaction higher than those who do not. Share your feelings and thoughts and hopes. People who hold things inside tend to feel isolated and misunderstood. Those who share feel both supported and more content, even if events do not go exactly as they wish. If you don't explain to other people what is important to you, how can they really understand you?

The power of synergy

Synergy is achieved when two or more people work together to create a better solution than they could if they worked alone. Synergy is not about *your* way, thinking you are always right, tolerating differences or working independentl: synergy is about celebrating differences, teamwork, open-mindedness, and finding new and better ways of working.

Synergy is the reward for thinking win-win. If you have ever been on a team, or in a play or in a band, and things came together, you have felt it. Great teams are usually made up of different types of individuals, each with something to offer the group. Each member brings his or her talents and contributes in a different way. Let's say you are listening to a piece of music. All the voices and instruments may be singing and playing at once, but they aren't competing. Individually the voices and instruments make different sounds and pause at different times, yet they blend together to create a harmonised sound. This is synergy.

There are lots of successful independent people, but look closely and you will see that behind their success there is synergy. Take great sports figures. In order for them to compete at the level they do there is always a team of people backing them: the coach, the publicist, the masseur, the physiotherapist, the accountant, and so on. Each one of these concentrates on what they are good at, and that in turn allows the competitor to be the best that he or she can possibly be.

Synergy is a process

The foundation is learning to celebrate differences. Some people shun diversity; others don't shun it but don't embrace it either. As we saw in secret 1, lucky people celebrate and value differences. They see them as an advantage, not a weakness. They know that two people who think differently can achieve more than two people who think alike. They know that celebrating doesn't meant you agree, only that you value. We are all unique. We learn differently, see differently, have different styles, traits and characteristics. Instead of trying to blend in and be like everyone else, lucky people aren't prejudiced by ignorance, clichés and labelling and are willing to consider all options on their way to finding the best solution for all concerned.

To build synergy you have to define the problem or opportunity. Then you need to share your ideas and try to understand the ideas of others. Then you create new options and ideas, and after brainstorming for a while the best idea will usually surface. But it takes a lot of maturity to get to synergy. You have to be willing to give and take. You need to work as part of a team. You need to listen, really listen, to other people's points of view and have the courage to express your own. And you need to do all this with an open mind that allows everyone's creative juices to flow.

Lucky people are always dripping with synergy. While they concentrate on what they are good at, they gather a team around them who focus on what they are good at. And everyone shares in the result, which is success, harmony, satisfaction, and, of course, luck.

GIVING TOO MUCH

You have probably heard at some time or another the advice that only after you love yourself can you love someone else. The same applies to giving. Only after you know how to give to yourself can you give to others.

Common sense and scientific research agree that until you have met your own physical and emotional needs you can't muster sufficient resources for someone else. When you start to neglect yourself for the sake of other people, you simply can't be effective in helping them.

Should you reach a point when you are exhausted with giving and taking responsibility for others it is absolutely crucial that you learn how to take care of yourself so that you are at your best, physically, mentally, and emotionally. If you are exhausted and resentful because you are giving too much or have too much responsibility, you will block luck from your life, because anger and negative thoughts infiltrate your mind or you are just too tired to seize opportunities.

There is generosity and there is stupidity. You don't want to be giving to people who are lazy or perpetuating their self-destruction. When lucky people give assistance their help isn't random. They think carefully about who they are going to help. This isn't because they are expecting something in return. What inspires them is knowing that their gift will be appreciated and valued.

Creating luck requires both a giving nature and self-love. You need to be able to take care of yourself. Give to others by all means, but not to the point where you are neglecting your own needs. Luck-making requires you to consider yourself as well—not just as an afterthought but all the time.

TAKE CARE OF YOURSELF

Now that we have established how important it is to take care of yourself before you can take care of others, think about the ways you take care of and strengthen yourself. What are your secret pleasures? What makes you feel good? Do you give yourself regular breaks and time off? Do you treat yourself? Do you stay connected to your friends and loved ones? How do you keep yourself healthy?

Lucky people have learned how important self-care is for their well-being, so they integrate it in their lives. There are lots of ways to help you take care of yourself, and each of us must find what works, but the following five self-care suggestions have been supported by scientific research as sure-fire ways to feel good about yourself.

EAT SOME FRUIT EVERY DAY

> Fruit-eaters feel good about what they eat, are less interested in eating junk food, and ultimately feel better about themselves. Keep fruit in the house and eat it as a snack. It's easy, it's cheap, it requires no preparation time, and it's good for you. Our bodies crave sweet tastes, but it is only in modern times, when sugary sweets have become available to us, that our taste for sweets has led to poor health. Eating fruit[46] is associated with a number of positive life habits that contribute to health and happiness, and eating more fruit is associated with a greater likelihood of feeling capable and satisfied.

Exercise

People who exercise—whether that involves an intense work-out or just a regular long walk—feel healthier, feel better about themselves, and enjoy their life more. Research[47] on physical activity finds that exercise increases self-confidence. Regular exercise, including brisk walking, directly increases happiness and can indirectly make a dramatic contribution to improving self-image.

Satisfactory sleep

Get a good night's sleep. A full night's rest is fuel for the next day. Rested people work better and are more comfortable when the day is over. Studies[48] show that quality and quantity of sleep contribute to health, well-being, and a positive outlook. For those who sleep less than eight hours, every hour of sleep results in an 8 per cent less positive feeling about their day. Too much sleep, say more than twelve hours, can also be unhelpful.

Good smells

Good smells awaken the senses and the brain and at a subconscious level remind us of good things. Research[49] shows that pleasant smells evoke surprise and happiness, while unpleasant smells trigger disgust and unhappy reactions. Here's a quick way to feel good about yourself. Air out your house and add some fragrant flowers. Make your home smell nice and you will feel the benefits.

Cultivate friendships

'True happiness is of a retired nature and an enemy to pomp and noise; it arises, in the first place, from the enjoyment of one's self and, in the next from the friendship and conversation of a few select companions.' (Joseph Addison)

If you want to know whether people are happy, don't ask them about how much money they have in the bank: ask them about their relationships. Researchers have identified the core factors in a happy life. The primary components are closeness of friends and family and relationships with fellow workers and neighbours. Together these features explain about 70 per cent of personal happiness.[50] Take advantage of opportunities to make friends. We need to feel we are part of something bigger, that we care about others and others care about us in return. Close friendships are one of the most meaningful factors in personal happiness, according to one study. If you feel close to other people you are four times as likely to feel good about yourself than if you did not feel close to anyone.[51]

Go and visit your neighbour. Neighbours are not only a potential source of friendship, they make us feel more comfortable in the place where we spend most of our time: home. Research[52] shows that greater community interactions can increase happiness significantly. Developing common interests with your friends and loved ones can make you feel that your bonds are much deeper than otherwise. Studies[53] reveal that each common interest between people in a relationship increases the likelihood of a lasting relationship and results in an increase of life satisfaction.

It isn't only friendships of a human kind that can help us feel good about ourselves. Research[54] shows that interaction with animals supplies us with both immediate joy and long-term positive feelings and contributes strongly to our happiness. Those with a loved pet are more likely to feel satisfied than those without.

Don't feel guilty about receiving

Some people find it very hard to accept generosity. There is the misguided belief that receiving puts you in a vulnerable position.

It is easier to be in the position of giver, creating indebtedness, than feeling indebted. It is easy to put up a wall and pretend to be self-sufficient. That way you don't have to know that you have needs or face the possibility that someone will disappoint you. Relying on other people can make you feel out of control.

As we saw in secret 1, to create luck good planning isn't enough. You also need to be flexible, spontaneous, and vulnerable. To expand your network of contacts you need to let yourself be given to. Remember, it isn't always about you. Other people have just as much need to give and help as you do. Why not let other people feel good about themselves by receiving and being grateful when help is being offered to you?

If you have problems with receiving, ask yourself why and how you are blocking good things from happening to you. What is threatening to you about receiving? Why do you prefer to be the giver? What happened to you to make you shun receiving? What short-term benefits does shutting off give you? What can you do today to open yourself more towards receiving love, connections and help from other people?

Luck is always knocking on the door, but it won't come to you unless you open it and are willing to let it in.

Take action today to balance giving and receiving

1. Begin each day by promising to do at least one thing that will make someone else feel good: offer someone a compliment, bring some flowers to a friend, or leave a bigger than normal tip when you eat out. If you are working with someone, give that person lots of thanks and credit.

2. Accept loving and generous behaviour from others. Other people have a need to give too. Receiving from others may make you feel vulnerable, but to create luck you need to be receptive and spontaneous. Say thank you when someone pays you a compliment; don't deny it. Allow other people to spoil

you if they want to. Stop feeling guilty about receiving; enjoy it.

3. Think of a lucky break you got in your life that goes back to an act of giving, though not directly from the moment you gave. Perhaps it happened much later; perhaps that person connected you to someone else who became your lucky charm; or perhaps the act of giving changed you in some way. By undergoing a transformation you were attracted to new circumstances that brought something good into your life.

4. Every community has countless opportunities for you to give of yourself. Be a reading tutor. Give your time to help a local charity shop. Anything you can do will not only help others but will help you. Volunteers feel good about themselves. They have a sense of purpose, feel appreciated, and are less likely to be bored. Volunteers experience rewards that cannot be attained in any other way. Even if you do not have a lot of time or skills, find an hour a month and give yourself to a good cause.

5. When you meet someone with a disability or impairment, don't feel sorry for them or avoid them; go out of your way to become acquainted. Listen to what they have to say; see the world through their eyes. Find ways to make their lives easier.

6. Share a problem with a friend you trust and see if exchanging viewpoints leads to new insights and ideas.

7. The next time you buy a present for a loved one, think about what they would like, not what you think they should get.

8. Cook yourself and someone you care about a healthy, nutritious meal.

9. Go out and treat yourself to something you really want: a book, a film, a new outfit, a haircut. Whatever it is, make sure it is something that makes you feel good.

13

USE YOUR INTUITION

To create more luck you must learn to work with your intuition. Intuition is a powerful tool that can help you recognise and achieve the happiness and success you want. It also helps you take advantage of coincidences—those seemingly random events that turn out to have more meaning than you expected.

Keyword: Insight

Whatever you call it—hunch, vibes, insight, foreboding, revelation, or inner voice—there is a little-used but powerful tool at your command that can help you improve your luck. It is your own untapped and often overlooked but highly effective intuitive system.

You can't explain why, but you have this gut feeling. This familiar feeling can, if used wisely, influence your luck. Did you ever have a hunch that something is going to happen and more often than not this hunch turned out to be correct? Whether you know it or not, your intuition is at work. What do we mean by intuition? *Webster's Dictionary* defines it as the act by which the mind perceives the truth about things immediately and without reasoning or deduction.

Intuition is knowing something without being aware of how you know it. It is an insight that seems to come from nowhere, a sudden knowledge without any logical evidence. Intuition can be heard as a voice in your head, or it can be a feeling that you need to take it easy or press ahead even if you are afraid. It leaves you feeling that you know something, even though you don't know why you know, and there is no rational explanation. It can be soft and gentle, or it can give you a very strong message. Some people think of intuition as their god speaking to them or the wise part of themselves directing them.

In this chapter we'll briefly explore the intuitive power of truth without reason. It could hold an answer to the mystery of why some of us are luckier than others.

Can you train your intuition?

It's clear that intuition plays an important role in some people's ability to avoid bad luck. If we could all know what the right thing to do in the future was, of course our luck would change. Imagine how brilliant it would be to play the stock market! Many of us wish we could have such powers. Is it really possible to develop intuition to a degree where it can be used for guidance in practical matters in everyday life? Can it be used to create luck? Psychologists believe that it can.

Many artists, writers, painters and inventors depend on the power of their intuition to amaze the world with their brilliant innovations. Thomas Edison firmly believed that some of his great inventions came from an idea outside himself. When struggling with a problem he would consider all the angles and then put the matter aside. Sooner or later a flash of insight would give him the solution.

Some people are more intuitive than others and receive flashes of insight frequently, while others experience them rarely. There is growing evidence, however, that most of us possess this ability to some degree. For example, our subconscious mind often tries to warn us when we are in danger. In a split second an impulse tells us to do something—run, fight, hide, look up, duck—and in many instances this impulse saves our life.

Hunches are conclusions based on knowledge we have gained

in the past. So the more knowledge you have in a chosen field, the more likely you are to experience those hunches. Many of us are intuitive in relation to our work, our intuition having developed over the years, or in a long-term relationship when we know what our partner is thinking without them saying anything.

Sometimes we wish our intuition would tell us what to do, but intuitive powers can't be switched on and off, and any attempt to do this is futile. Hunches flash into our unconscious unbidden, often coming in the form of an inner awareness or a definite idea of what we should do, gently nudging us in the right direction.

We have more hunches than we realise. Many times when our intuition speaks we don't recognise it. To improve our chances of luck we need to be sensitive to this higher intelligence and maintain an open-minded attitude of expectant receptivity that helps us recognise intuitive urges when they appear. Otherwise they could slip away unnoticed.

Your subconscious mind

In order to learn the skills that will enable you to tap in to your intuition, it is first important to understand how your subconscious works.

We have two distinct systems of awareness: conscious and intuitive. Each system records, thinks, feels and remembers in its own way. The conscious mind records the signals received by the five senses—seeing, hearing, smelling, touching, and tasting—and organises them in a logical sequence. The intuitive mind picks up another set of signals. It stores this information continually in a vast storehouse of unconscious memories—information you can use whether you know it or not. The subconscious mind is always trying to bring information to your attention through symbols, dreams, and feelings. Unfortunately it is often ignored, derided, or rejected. This is to your detriment and frustrates your ability to create good luck.

Have you ever had this experience? 'It's right on the tip of my tongue,' but you can't quite remember. Later, seemingly from nowhere, the name or the thought arrives. Here you have a classic example of your subconscious working. By consciously trying to remember and then forgetting about it, you trigger a search in your subconscious mind. When you are struggling with a problem, try this:

> Gather all the information you can about the problem. Then concentrate intensely on all the possible angles. Really work at trying to find the best solution, and turn the matter over and over in your mind.
>
> Then let go. Completely stop thinking about it. Turn your attention to something else. The problem will slip into your subconscious mind, where it will be processed and filed away. It is now that your intuition gets to work scanning all the information you have stored and making new connections. Then right out of the blue a solution will present itself.
>
> A good time to let your subconscious mind solve your problem is while you are asleep. If you happen to wake in the night, make sure you have a pen and paper handy to write down your solution. After you go to bed concentrate on the problem, considering all the angles. Limit yourself to thinking about one thing as you lie down to sleep. If other thoughts start to intrude, guide them back to that one subject. Too many thoughts are unsettling and make it harder for us to fall asleep by putting us on edge. At this time just before sleep your subconscious mind is at its peak receptivity. While you are asleep it will scan your data banks for a solution.
>
> The answer may pop into your mind during the night or in the morning, or it may take longer. Remember, you can't force the process. Don't be discouraged. Keep repeating the technique, and sooner or later when you are relaxed and thinking about something else the answer will pop into your

mind. You may find this hard to accept, but try it. It really works.

How to develop your intuition

To develop your intuition you need to think constructively and optimistically. Worry and frustration will inhibit the process. Replace those negative thoughts with positive ones, and stimulate your mind with reading and conversation.

Broaden your horizons by networking with people from various backgrounds and with a variety of viewpoints. This will stretch your mind and give you fresh ideas. Don't rebel against these ideas. Keep an open mind and find time to be quiet. Your intuition is more accessible when the pace is slow and peaceful. If your life is busy, stressful, and cluttered with constant to-do's, the distractions may be too loud for your intuition to be heard. Sometimes to compete with these distractions your intuition will get louder and louder, and you may not like what it has to say. For example, if you ignore warnings to take care of yourself your body may revolt and slow you down by force with a bout of sickness.

Some people find that daily meditation helps, or yoga, or tai chi, or other activities designed to calm your mind. Take some quiet time to yourself away from distractions, such as television, radio, or noisy children, and use it to think, imagine, and dream. Set aside time each day for a break of some kind. Tuning in to your thoughts for just ten or fifteen minutes of quiet time each day can make all the difference in helping you connect with your intuitive powers.

If you want to find what is right for you, your subconscious mind will provide you with the answers, so concentrate on what you want. Don't let your logical mind come up with all the answers, and don't try to force the process. Instead, be patient and use your intuition gradually and carefully. And as you start listening to those hunches an amazing thing will start to happen: your luck will improve.

EXERCISES TO ENTICE YOUR INTUITION

- Gaze at the sky and the slow-moving clouds. This can create a restful atmosphere that helps intuition to surface.
- Ease gently into a hot bath until you are submerged except for your face. Allow all directed thought to leave your mind. Close your eyes and listen as your intuition takes centre stage.
- If you are a passenger, look out the window at the passing scenery. Allow your unconscious tension to fall away. Concentrate on your breathing, relax, and permit random thoughts to float through your mind. Defer all judgments of the thoughts. The drone of the engine, the swish of the wheels or the clacking of the train's wheels can serve as soothing background noise while you permit your intuition to dominate.
- Gaze at the seashore. Listen to the lapping of the waves. Breathe for deep relaxation with your eyes open or closed. Try to get a feeling for the infinity of life as encompassed in the eternal motion of the sea. Some people become mesmerised watching the rhythmic movement of the waves. In this state of peaceful observation your intuition has an opportunity to be heard.
- Listen to music. A positive effect on mood was found in the majority of individuals[55] when they listened to their favourite music. This form of relaxation can help us feel more at ease, happy, and in touch with our intuition.

HOW TO RECOGNISE INTUITION

Intuition speaks a different language from the one we use in daily life. The first awareness many of us have of our intuitive system is in feelings. Every feeling has a cause, and when it has no apparent cause you must look for an intuitive answer. Feelings and moods are the basic language of intuition. Have you ever felt afraid when there was no reason to? Have you ever felt angry when you didn't know why? Have you ever felt alone when you were in a group of people? In each case your intuitive system is trying to reach you. In dealing with our feelings we need to be scientific and notice connections between events. Our intuition can help us make sense of things and create a pattern. If you don't understand why you are feeling a certain way, you can't do anything to change your world. Research shows that those who are least likely to overcome feelings of disaffection with life are those who cannot define the source of their feelings.[56]

Think about your emotions and feelings, and let your intuition guide you. Then, even when you feel unhappy you can take comfort in knowing the cause and doing something about it.

> When Mark, her on-off boy-friend, handed Jenny a bunch of flowers she got very angry. Why? It took some time before Jenny realised: on many occasions flowers had symbolised goodbyes to her. Both her parents had died when she was still in her teens, and her best friend was killed in a car crash. For each occasion the floral tributes stuck in Jenny's mind. Many of them were from people who didn't really care for her parents or her friend at all and were simply for convention's sake. When she got angry with Mark's gift, it was because she was concerned that he too might be false and not give her the love and appreciation she deserved. If she had not stopped to try to understand the message behind her feelings she might never have identified her problem. Instead, she discussed her problem with Mark, and he was quick to make amends and give their relationship the honesty and commitment she needed.

Dreams are one of the most important voices of the intuitive system, because the conscious mind is recessive in sleep and the non-verbal mind dominates. The most favourable conditions for receiving intuitive messages are during periods of quiet and serenity, when logic is subdued or shut down. This is what happens in sleep.

Your intuition may come to you clearly, or it may come to you in a dream with symbolic and metaphorical undertones. Keep a notebook and record your dreams, and you may notice a connection between animals, people or events that crop up in them and decisions you are trying to make. Don't worry about books that claim to interpret dreams. What matters is how you interpret the images. What is your intuition trying to communicate to you through your subconscious mind? Watch for puns and allegories; the subconscious mind has a sense of humour too. Seeing a cat may remind you of independence, a dog of loyalty. Finding a coin may make you feel reassured if coins have a special significance in your life. It is the significance you give things that matters and the confidence they give you to move forward beyond fear.

You may physically manifest a message from your intuition. I always get headaches when I am stressed. You may hear certain expressions or recommendations several times, and this may lead you to act on them. Or things that have a special significance for you, like a certain piece of music or a special food, may come into your life when you need to feel supported, giving you peace of mind and courage. Your intuition may also speak to you in sections: a little bit now, a little bit more a few days later. It is only when you have all the pieces of the puzzle that things start to have clarity.

If you still aren't sure how your intuition speaks to you, carry a pen and paper around with you and jot down thoughts that come to you randomly that you think could be your intuition talking. They don't have to be earth-shattering, just simple thoughts that come to you out of the blue when you are walking to the shops or cooking dinner.

Don't make any judgments or decisions; just write the thoughts down. At the end of the day review what you have written and see if a pattern emerges.

Identify your questions

You can't get an answer if you don't have a question. Often our intuition doesn't speak to us because we are asking the wrong questions. If you ask the wrong question you either get no answer at all or get one that is hard to understand. So how do you ask your intuition questions?

Keep your questions short, simple, and specific. 'Should I take the job from company X?' not 'Show me the kind of job I should be looking for.' Start practising with questions that don't really matter that much. If the doorbell rings, ask your intuition who it is. If the phone rings, do the same. Have fun with this and see if you can improve your accuracy. Then move on to more important things. If you get an intuitive flash you don't quite understand, ask for clarity.

The more questions you ask, the more you can come to expect your intuition to have answers for you.

Trust a hunch—or not

Some unfortunate incidents, like being driven off the road by a drunk driver or being caught in a violent storm, are simply being in the wrong place at the wrong time. Other examples of bad luck could be linked to ignoring clear warning signs from your intuition.

What if you decide to take a job, knowing it isn't a match for your career aspirations? You turn up at work each morning with a knot in your stomach. Is it bad luck that you were fired six months later? What if you know you are taking on too many commitments? Is it bad luck that you aren't able to meet them? What if your intuition told you not to trust someone and you ignored it, and six months later they let you down?

Your intuition is a gift that can bring you luck, success, and happiness. You owe it to yourself to pay attention to it. It might help to think about all the times your intuition was screaming at you to do something that you ignored. Why did you ignore it, and, in hindsight, what were the consequences of ignoring it? What were your reasons? Were you afraid of looking stupid, being wrong, hurting someone's feelings, making a change, losing money? Did other people change your mind, or did you think changing your mind would cause too much trouble for other people? Were you just too lazy? Could you hear your intuition speaking? Or don't you trust your intuition?

Distinguish between intuition and fear

How do you know whether it is your intuition speaking or fear? When the inner alarm sounds, is it a test of your courage that you need to do something you fear or because you need to stop something you have already planned?

If you are willing to be honest with yourself, you will know the difference between fear and intuition. Let's say you are about to get married and doubts creep in about whether you have made the right decision. Is this pre-wedding jitters, or are you really making a mistake? If it is a mistake, you have probably had these doubts all along and there will be feelings of dread. You will feel as if you are just going through the motions, and the feeling of dread will get worse when the wedding is over. If this is the right decision the panic feels different. It will be mixed up with love and respect for your partner and will disappear soon after the wedding. You would be able to talk to your partner about it and feel reassured. You will feel scared without doubting that you have made the right decision.

Say you haven't reached the wedding stage yet but you are apprehensive about the relationship. If the relationship isn't right for you, you will probably feel quite anxious most of the time. If the relationship is right, mixed in with the apprehension will be moments of true calm and happiness. You will be able to talk to your partner about your fears when they occur and be reassured.

Another way to distinguish between fear and intuition is that intuition is a lot quieter than fear. When you know something intuitively you know it without a lot of words to explain it, even if it is illogical. When you are fearful, there are long-drawn-out explanations that clatter around in your head—anything but a quiet knowing of the truth.

Intuition is also a lot gentler than fear. If the thoughts in your mind are full of shame, anxiety, and judgment, they are likely to originate from your conscious mind. Intuition tends to be warmer, gentler, kinder, and non-judgmental. Fear tends to demotivate you into inaction; intuition guides you gently in the right direction. If the voices in your head say you are a loser, you always quit, you can't do what it takes, it isn't your intuition that is talking. Your intuition might tell you that something doesn't feel right, that this isn't the right thing for you, that it's time to move on, change direction, and find what works better for you. There may be no words at all, just a gut feeling that it is time to make a change

INTUITION AT WORK

Much economic success depends on what appears to be luck. Chance-taking is an intrinsic part of the business world. Fashion designers anticipate the next season's trends; publishers anticipate what the public want to read, and so on. Some business people seem to get it right time and time again. They keep taking chances and winning. It is not just luck. The intuitive factor gives them a powerful edge. They have the ability to calculate the odds based on information processed at an intuitive level.

> 'When it comes down to the long record and the hard facts, you are your own luck. What we ordinarily call luck may really be a bit of chance—something unprepared and unexpected —but usually there's more to it than that. I think it is partly intuition which is a kind of thinking that goes on when we aren't aware of it, when we aren't consciously

> working on thinking. I believe too that it is a sense of timeliness you develop that tells you when to make your move.' (Herman W. Lay, former president of Frito-Lay)
>
> 'I strongly believe in the validity of intuition as a guide to action, especially in imponderable, difficult situations. Many times I have made a decision I just had a feeling about it. Usually these decisions turned out to be right.' (Bill Clinton)

Gather all the information you can, use your judgment, and even if the choice is now obvious check your intuition before you make your move. If your intuition says no when reason and judgment say yes, wait, gather more data, and consider your choices again. If your intuition says yes, go ahead. Success favours the chance-takers. Nothing ventured, nothing gained. Timidity does not make for progress or happiness.

SYNCHRONICITY

At one time or another most of us have experienced strange or inexplicable things: someone rings when you are thinking of them; a letter arrives with exactly the information you need that day; we sit beside someone on a train who turns out to be important for our future.

The word *synchronicity* was invented by the Swiss psychologist Carl Jung, who brought the idea of meaningful coincidence to public attention. If you can learn to read the signs of synchronicity, the luckier you will get. When you ask for help, it will only be a matter of time before a sign appears. When you need support to take the next step on your journey through life, that support will come.

Stories of amazing coincidences from everyday life fill us with a sense of awe and remind us that the world can be a magical place.

A woman leaned out of her apartment window in New York and screamed for help. She was trapped in her bathroom. The inside doorknob had fallen off when her youngest child, aged two, had closed the door on the other side. Two other children, aged three and four, were in the kitchen alone as supper was being cooked. The woman alternated between trying to break down the door and shouting to be heard. She was beginning to give up hope.

Meanwhile, a young man who lived twenty miles away happened to be visiting the district. Within moments he was outside the bathroom door and giving instructions to the woman to put her fingers in the hole where the knob should be. He told her to lift the door slightly and quickly pull it open. The door opened. It happened that this man had lived in the woman's apartment for fifteen years. He knew how to enter the front door without a key, and because the bathroom knob kept falling off when he lived there, he had learned how to open it.

Think of all those people you have met in a random, coincidental way who either helped you when you needed it most or changed your life in a pivotal way. One of the most common occurrences of a meaningful coincidence is the manner in which we find partners. When you consider the billions of people on this planet, isn't it a miracle that some of us do find our soulmate?

BELIEVE IT OR NOT: A TRUE STORY

One summer evening Cathy set out on a blind date. She didn't have much faith in it amounting to anything, but having agreed to it she wanted to keep her word. She had been told to look for a blue car and for a driver called John who would be wearing a blue shirt. They were to meet at eight o'clock outside the local post office. At a couple of minutes past eight John arrived. Cathy was pleasantly surprised.

> After the film and before dinner John asked her how she knew Bob. 'Who is Bob?' Cathy asked. 'What do you mean, who is Bob? Bob is the one who set us up,' John replied. Cathy was confused. Jim had set them up. John didn't know who Jim was. After a few more who's and what's and what are you talking about, the puzzle was solved. They realised that another couple must have made arrangements to meet at exactly the same time and place. They were out with the wrong date. Without hesitating a moment, John told Cathy that he was having a great time and he wanted it to continue. Cathy agreed. It is now ten years later and they are happily married with two sons, whom they decided to call Bob and Jim.

Sometimes in our life all we have to do is show up, be present, and allow the magic to happen. Cathy and John's story is a great example of both magic and creating luck. If either of them had been rigid about keeping to the plans designed by their friends, they may never have become a couple. Having conviction and plans is essential for luck-making, but following the flow of our intuition can seal the deal.

Whether it is as simple as anticipating a phone call or as dramatic as finding a lost love, what you experience could have more significance than you think. To increase your awareness and understanding of the power of meaningful coincidences in your life, think of some encounters, meetings or events that have affected you positively. Once you have listed them, look for actions that made them possible. These coincidences did not create luck for you. It was the way you responded when they occurred that brought you luck.

Being too stubborn or rigid about what we want can be detrimental. Without a doubt a solid belief in your own abilities increases your chances of happiness,[57] but believing in yourself means thinking you are a capable person, not that you will never make a mistake. Don't let your ego get in the way of your free will. Don't think that you cannot learn from others or that you should never change your plans. Studies[58] show that when a person is convinced they are correct and not open to suggestions, disagreements and unhappiness within relationships are likely.

MAKE YOUR COINCIDENCES MEANINGFUL

Delight in the fact that sometimes you are not the one in control of your life, and feel reassured by this. 'Meaningful coincidences are manifestations of an all-embracing universal order,' writes Arthur Koestler in *The Roots of Coincidence*. Surrendering to a different agenda from the one you created means giving up the pretence that you have complete control over your life.

Something must always be left to chance. If everything could be planned and nothing unexpected ever happened, the world would be the dullest place that could be conceived. We are all at the mercy of circumstances beyond our control. There will always be things that happen in life we can't understand or explain. It's just fate, we say. When confronted with the unexpected, we can either throw up our hands in despair and blame chance or do what lucky people do and interpret daily events as meaningful and guided rather than random.

Neither view is right or wrong, but since you get to choose your beliefs, why not believe in a philosophy that gives you greater hope? Why not believe in the idea that things happen for a reason? Why not believe that things aren't always what they seem? Why not believe in the impossible? Why not believe that the universe is really a magical place?

Life would be very dull indeed without coincidence. The chance meeting, the life-saving encounter, the lost object that suddenly reappears—all seem to be the work of an unseen power. Some coincidences grow legends around them, and explanations abound about why they happened, but lucky people who have experienced the irrational force of coincidences know that there is no reason. Sometimes good or bad things happen that can't be explained. All we can do is respond appropriately, turn the situation to our advantage, and believe that miracles can happen.

TAKE ACTION TODAY TO DEVELOP YOUR INTUITION

1. To get in touch with your intuition you need quiet time away from distractions to tune in. Take small steps. Try turning off the television and radio. Let the answering-machine take messages. Set the alarm an hour earlier, and make time to meditate or just have a cup of coffee and think.

2. Intuition communicates in a language different from the chit-chat of every day. Your intuition may come to you in a dream with symbolic messages, or through animals or other people—seeing a butterfly reminds you of new beginnings—or through your body—a headache means you are getting stressed out. Carry a journal around with you, and jot down thoughts that come to you that you think may be your intuition talking.

3. Practise when the phone rings. Who is that calling? Have fun seeing if you can improve your accuracy.

4. Ask your intuition specific, focused questions, and watch for the answer. It may show up in the form of an amazing coincidence or a thought in your head or someone phoning you to give you the information you need.

5. Listen to your favourite piece of instrumental music. Set the volume a little lower than usual and close your eyes, suspend judgment, stop all directed thought and simply listen. Let the music become background noise, and let random thoughts drift in and out of your mind. Make no attempt to control them. When the music has finished review your experience,

particularly the imagery that drifted through your mind and the feelings you experienced while you listened. What do these images mean to you?

6. Find a quiet place and close your eyes. As you breathe, let your thoughts drop away. Now concentrate on your breathing and shed all other thoughts. If you find it hard to concentrate, make a note of the number of times you breathe. Set a goal of fifty to a hundred cycles. This will help you relax and make you feel ready to let subtle feelings and fleeting visions pass through your half-awake mind.

7. Just before you are about to drift off to sleep, think of one particular thing. When you waken up the next morning record your thoughts. Did your intuition speak in the night through dreams?

8. Choose your favourite picture or photograph and study every detail. Close your eyes and visualise that picture or photograph in your mind's eye. Now imagine that you are taking a walk inside that picture. What do you see? What do you hear? What do you smell? Open your eyes and look at your picture again. Do you notice anything new about it?

9. At the end of the day remember your day backwards. It sounds easy but it isn't. The instinct will be to remember things from beginning to end. This is a very powerful and challenging mental exercise that can help you get in touch with your intuition, so try it for five to ten seconds at first and build up from there.

14

Turn Rejection into Resolve

Lucky people aren't those who have never been rejected, let down or disappointed in their life: quite the opposite. In fact the most successful people are often the ones who have suffered most disappointments. Setbacks are going to happen in your life. Lucky people spend little time feeling disappointed. Instead, they get back to work making luck out of any change of plans.

Keyword: Resilience

If you have goals and go after them you will find luck—but not every time. There will be moments when, no matter how hard you try, all you get is no, no, no. This is when it is easy to panic, get depressed, or give up. Lucky people approach things a little differently. Whenever they are confronted by something that seems bigger and tougher than they are and the standard way of confronting it doesn't work, they look to their ingenuity.

When both my agents told me that it was time to slow down my writing career, I was devastated. I didn't want to slow down. I had finally found something I wanted to do. I went back to teaching for a while, but a small part of me couldn't accept that this was the end. I had to give it a go. I decided to be bold, cut out the middle man, and approach publishers directly with my ideas instead of running them past my agents first. What did I have to lose? They could only say no.

> So I approached all the editors I had worked for before with several ideas I was yearning to write about. Many said no, but one said yes. And that is how this book was born.

To improve your chances of luck you need initiative and get-up-and-go when life gives you a thumbs-down. This may be hard, especially if you are used to following rules and accepting what other people say or waiting for things to happen, but it is well worth the effort in the end.

The road to success is paved with failure

Have you ever wondered why lucky people seem to bounce back from setbacks, while others crumple up at the slightest let-down? It is because lucky people know how to use rejection as a stepping-stone to success.

'No' is an awful word to hear. It can make you cry, scream, be nasty to your children, bury your head under the covers, sleep until noon, eat a whole box of chocolates, or sit in a stupor watching daytime television. Funny, though, you'd think we would be used to disappointment by now. It is estimated that by the time we're eighteen we have probably heard the word 'no' at least 150,000 times. Setbacks are going to happen in life. Some things don't work out the way we want them to. So what should you do when doors slam shut in your face? How do you motivate yourself when you hear the big no? You find ways to turn rejection into direction?

Don't take it personally

When things go wrong we tend to lay the blame on ourselves. Psychologists at the National Institute of Mental Health find that many of us fall victim to the everything-is-my-fault approach to life. Two things we often overlook are how little we directly control a situation and how little value there is in spending time blaming ourselves. These thoughts do not fix the problem or make anything better. Blame is about the past. A plan of action to fix a problem is about the future. The truth is that some things are in our control and some are not.

Although it is important to accept the part you played when setbacks occur, don't delude yourself into thinking that disappointments are always your fault. Good or bad luck does not depend on how many good or bad things happen to you. What is more important is not making negative conclusions about yourself when things go wrong.

As we have seen, research shows that[59] people who think of themselves as the cause of negative events are far less likely to attract luck than those who do not. In a study of adult self-esteem, researchers found that people who are happy with themselves take defeat and explain it away, treating it as an isolated incident that indicates nothing about their ability. People who are unhappy take defeat and enlarge it, making it stand for who they are and using it to predict the future outcome of their life.[60] Rejection spells failure only if you do not believe in yourself. For those who believe in themselves, it is only a challenge.

Accept yourself as you are. Don't try to be perfect. You are just like everyone else: a mix of abilities and limitations. Accepting yourself does not mean ignoring your faults or not taking any responsibility: it means believing in your own value.

The hardest rejection to overcome is often self-rejection. Don't make things worse for yourself. Rejection is a fact of life. If you can see clearly where you went wrong—say you weren't prepared enough for your driving test, or you applied for a job for which you weren't qualified—use that information and move on. But if you don't know what you did wrong, stop thinking that everything is your fault. Have you ever felt hurt when you waved frantically to a friend across the street and he or she seemed to ignore you? What if your friend forgot to put in her contact lenses and simply didn't see you? Sometimes disagreements with partners, friends and family or disappointments at work have nothing to do with what you have said or done.

Ask why

Whenever you hear 'no', do everything you can to find out why. Zero in on the reason you didn't get what you want, so that you can deal with it, if possible, or move on to the next objective.

Reflecting on life's disappointments helps you discover other ways to improve your luck. How fast you are able to work through this self-evaluation and move on with your life determines the quality of your luck. You need to learn from your mistakes, not become obsessed with them.

The next time you are rejected, try to find out why. The answer could help you change your approach. If, for example, you have been rejected for a job, say something non-threatening like 'I appreciate your getting back to me. It would be very helpful to my future career if you could tell me why you chose someone else.' Perhaps you just needed more experience, a better reference, or another qualification. Then you can try again, using what you have discovered.

Focus on the positive

Stop viewing setbacks as failures. If life gives you a lemon, make lemonade. Put a positive spin on rejection. This doesn't mean you won't feel sad or disappointed. Of course you will. It means you make the most of wherever you are and acknowledge that getting through the tough times will help you learn and grow as a human being.

If a relationship ends, see the break-up as an opportunity, a catalyst for moving on and changing your life for the better. If a friend declines an invitation, focus on the friends who have accepted. Don't allow rejection to devastate you. However negative a situation seems, there is always something positive you can focus on.

Think of *no* as meaning 'Not this way; let's look for another, better way.' If a diet isn't working, seek advice from a dietician. If you don't get the promotion, consider other work opportunities.

If a business idea is rejected by one person, seek advice from someone else. Don't limit yourself to one way of getting what you want. Be ingenious. Try other approaches—even bold, not-the-way-it's-usually-done approaches. Just because something has never been done before doesn't mean you shouldn't try. Just because someone says you shouldn't doesn't mean you can't.

TRY, TRY, TRY AGAIN

> 'I'll never give up, for I may have a streak of luck before I die.'

Thomas Edison wrote these words to a friend. He was twenty-two at the time, and his work as an inventor was plagued with problems. 'No matter what I do, I reap nothing but trouble,' he wrote in the next letter. Edison was later to become one of the most prolific inventors in history, holding more than a thousand patents, including the light-bulb and the phonograph.

You only need one person to say yes. If at first you don't succeed, welcome to the club. You are in excellent company. The Beatles, Madonna, J. K. Rowling and John Grisham, to name but a few, all faced big failures when they started out. Many successful people with great ideas were rejected by everybody—except one. And it was that one acceptance that turned their fortunes around. It doesn't matter how many people say no if you can find one who says yes; you must simply keep searching for that one.

Being lucky means rising after each fall. We should worry less about failing and more about the chances we miss when we don't even try. Many of the people we admire failed many times. Albert Einstein didn't talk until he was four. Beethoven's music teacher said, 'As a composer he is hopeless.' You can't succeed unless you have the courage to fail. When Thomas Edison's experiments with a storage battery failed to produce good results, the inventor refused to concede defeat: 'I've just found 10,000 ways that won't work!'

Every lasting success involves overcoming rejection. When you adopt this attitude, rejection isn't so frightening any more. It is a step on the road to success. Be persistent in a creative way. If you truly want something, you will find ways to make it work. Don't give up. Believe in yourself. Keep looking for the house, the relationship, the job, the publisher, or whatever.

SOME LUCKY LOSERS

'Behind bad luck comes good luck' is a gypsy proverb. If you feel that life is passing you by and things aren't going your way, don't despair. You never know what the future holds. Remember, disappointments are an inevitable stepping-stone on the road to success. Consider these experiences:

> Harrison Ford failed philosophy in his senior year at university in Wisconsin and never received his degree. Following a 45-second role in his first film, *Dead Heat on a Merry Go Round*, a Columbia executive told him, 'You ain't got it, kid.' After bit parts in *Gunsmoke* and *The Virginian*, Ford quit acting for a while and became a carpenter. Later he became a superstar, starring in the *Star Wars* films and as Indiana Jones in the *Raiders of the Lost Ark* series. He also starred in *Blade Runner*, *Witness*, *Patriot Games*, *The Fugitive*, and *Air Force One*.
>
> The Beatles were rejected in 1962 by a Decca Records executive, Dick Rowe, who signed Brian Poole and the Tremoloes instead, following consecutive auditions by the two groups. The Beatles' Decca audition tape was subsequently turned down by Philips, Columbia, and HMV. They were finally offered a recording contract by the Parlophone producer George Martin, and they became the most influential rock-and-roll band in history.

> Walt Disney's first cartoon company, Laughogram, went bankrupt. He created Mickey Mouse and became the most famous name in film animation. He produced *Snow White and the Seven Dwarfs*, *Pinocchio*, *Fantasia*, *Bambi* and *Cinderella* and founded Disneyland.

> Martin Luther King Junior was forced at the age of fourteen to surrender his bus seat to a white passenger and to stand for the next ninety miles. King became leader of the American civil rights movement and delivered his famous 'I have a dream' speech on the steps of the Lincoln Memorial before an audience of more than 200,000 people in 1963. He was awarded the Nobel Peace Prize in 1964.

It is encouraging and inspiring to know that anyone who is anyone has had to look rejection in the face and spit in its eye. You can too. Everyone falls down. You are a failure only if you don't get back up.

Don't face your problems alone

We are social creatures and need to discuss our problems with others, whether it is those who care about us or those who have faced similar difficulties. When you are alone problems seem huge; when you share them you gain perspective and find solutions.

The only thing that hiding your problems does is make sure no-one helps you with them. If people don't know you need help, how can they help you?

> John was having trouble paying his mortgage. When he missed his first payment all kinds of things could have been done to help him. He had friends who could have told him the rules, who could have helped. He didn't ask. He was embarrassed and wanted to deal with his own problems. But he didn't know how to get himself out of trouble. He

> became more and more upset and isolated himself even more. Eventually, after missing his fourth mortgage payment, he was evicted.

An experiment was conducted with a group of women suffering from low self-esteem. Some were introduced to women with similar problems, and others were left to work things out on their own. Those who interacted with others showed a dramatic reduction in their problems. Those who were left alone showed no improvement.[61] Two heads are better than one. If something is worrying you, share your problem with someone you trust. Don't keep it to yourself.

Take a risk

We all like to stay in our comfort zone, where everything is familiar. It's easy and doesn't require too much effort. We feel safe and secure. New things make us feel nervous and uncomfortable. But this territory is the place to go for opportunity, the only place in which you can find luck. You'll never find it in your comfort zone, unless you want to lead a safe but boring life.

Taking a risk is always scary at first. Once you realise that you are not going off a cliff and that you are going to survive you become wiser and stronger, even if embracing the challenge was a mistake. Don't confuse risk with recklessness. Risk is about calculation and weighing up the odds before you take chances. Reckless behaviour is the absence of calculation.

Keep moving

Anything that moves you forward is good, even if it is anger. A 'Who needs you anyway' or 'It's your loss' attitude can be very positive. On the other hand anxiety, despondency and revenge are self-destructive. When you hear the word *no*, don't make rude phone calls, slash clothing, or sit in a depressed stupor. Instead, let rejection motivate you to get right back to work. *No* isn't the end of the world; it's information, and far better than being left wondering.

If something doesn't go according to plan or a relationship breaks down, tell yourself that no amount of self-pity and tears is going to change the situation or bring your partner back. Cry, swear, kick a punchbag for a few hours, and then stand up and tell yourself it's okay. *No* is bad. *No* stinks. But at least you know where you stand and you can start concentrating on what to do next. Think of this loss as a temporary setback, not a permanent problem. To get what you want in life you must keep moving, generating action and new opportunities.

Get busy

Nothing eases disappointment faster than new challenges. Whatever loss you have experienced, your suffering will be eased if you get busy. New challenges and accomplishments serve as distractions that stop obsessive thinking and help you rebuild whatever self-esteem you may have lost in over-analysing your disappointment.

This isn't to say you should ignore disappointment and heartache and bury yourself in work. Once you think through the problem and understand why it happened, you should take steps to occupy your mind. Otherwise negative thoughts will return and you'll start to put yourself down again.

When you feel like you are hitting a brick wall

Sometimes we have to acknowledge that, despite all our best efforts, we can't have what we want. The man or woman of your dreams turns out to be a nightmare or isn't interested in us, the perfect job opportunity slips out of your hands, you aren't ever going to squeeze into a size 10 pair of jeans, and so on. When that happens we need to accept that life isn't going according to our plan—but perhaps there is a better plan. You are either on to something, about to learn a valuable lesson, or something much better lies ahead.

When you hit an obstacle and can't get past it, get curious about what the future holds. You never know what could be waiting around the corner. As soon as the cup empties, it can be filled with something better. That's the way the world works, if you believe it does.

Fascinating research on happiness reveals that people are about as happy as they think they are, regardless of status, wealth, or circumstances. How we regard misfortune to ourselves and others determines how we feel. If we say, 'This is a disaster; I can't accept this,' our pain intensifies. To create luck we need to grieve over our losses and then accept what has happened, however hard that may be. Acceptance doesn't mean you like it: it means you stop fighting what you cannot change. It means moving on. Sometimes when we are so closely involved in the events of our lives we can't see the bigger picture and how what is happening now can add to our growth.

Worry: the root of all bad and good luck

It is natural and normal for us to worry about rejection and failure. Biologically we are programmed to run away from danger. Although there are not as many reasons to do that any more, the survival instinct remains and has evolved into worrying. In other words, we mentally run away from things we fear may harm us.

We all have a tendency to jump to conclusions, to worry about *what if's*. But most of what we worry about never happens. We waste valuable energy on scenarios that will never transpire, energy we could have directed positively to create luck. If you are always exhausted in worrying about crises that never occur, you won't be able to harness your resources to get what you want. Whenever worry strikes, stop and wake yourself up to the reality that you are wasting your time. Worrying about things never achieves anything. It causes inaction and feelings of helplessness. Worry is the enemy of good luck.

Step back from your worry and use it as information. Whenever worry strikes, it indicates a problem that needs to be solved. Instead of resenting or fearing worry, be grateful that it alerts you to potential problem areas. Find out what is worrying you, and ask yourself if there is anything you can do. If the answer is no, accept that you can do nothing and that worrying won't help. It will waste your time and energy and make you feel worse. Let it go. If there is something you can do about what is worrying you, think what approaches can ease the situation, and take action. Perhaps what you are doing isn't the right thing, but at least you are experimenting to find the best solution. Lucky people replace worry with problem-solving.

Good judgment

Good judgment is all about fashioning your behaviour to minimise bad luck. Poor judgment is not being able to assess the repercussions of your actions. Good judgment requires us to ask two fundamental questions:

> What can I say or do that will help me get what I want?
> What impact will my actions have on other people?

Unlucky people don't ask themselves both these questions. They seem determined to repeat the same mistake over and over again and refuse to recall what it was that changed people's opinions of them and made them less willing to help. Those who stubbornly believe their approaches are right and everyone else is wrong suffer bad luck because of their obstinacy. The fact is that these people could often avoid rejection if they improved their judgment.

Good judgment will limit your chances of being rejected. Actively take steps to reduce the number of mistakes you make.

Learn as much as you can about the issues involved. Listen to as many knowledgeable people as possible before acting.

Think before you act. If you are willing to take the risk and you think the outcome is worth the fall-out, that's fine, as long as you are prepared for it. Ask yourself these questions:

> Do I have to act now?
> How will taking more time help?
> What do I want to say or do?
> Who will be affected?
> Who will be offended? Does it matter if they are?
> How can I offend the smallest number of people?
> If I can't avoid hurting people, how can I ease the pain?

Put yourself in other people's shoes to anticipate how they will respond. You may decide that what you need to say or do overrides their needs, but the fact that you have thought about it shows you are prepared and less likely to attract bad luck. If you aren't sure how people will react, use your common sense. The fastest way to become a people expert is to listen and watch.

Believe in your success

To view misfortune as an opportunity you must believe you will succeed. Your belief in yourself, especially in times of misfortune, will inspire others to believe in you also. If you demonstrate that you are a fighter and can handle misfortune, people will want to help you. If you give up at the first bump in the road, don't expect much assistance.

Limit more bad luck by counteracting it with behaviour that is irresistible. Don't complain. Keep believing in yourself so that others can too. In this way you attract the help that can turn your misfortune around and bring good luck in the future.

ACTIONS TO TAKE TODAY TO TURN REJECTION INTO RESOLVE

1. Are you noticing patterns in your life? Do similar mistakes or disappointments keep happening? Are you dating the wrong kind of person, arguing about the same issues with your children, not getting the jobs you apply for? Are you setting impossible standards for yourself? Gather as much information as you can and reconsider your approach. Then think how you can replace negative patterns with positive ones. Could you try dating the kind of person you never usually go out with? Could you try listening to your children instead of telling them what to do? Could you seek career advice to find out what would be the next-best step for you? Remind yourself that perfection is impossible and mistakes will happen. Even the happiest couples have arguments, the most successful people make mistakes, the most beautiful people have bad-hair days.

2. Without being unrealistic, write down in a special notebook ten things you want to achieve in the next twelve months. Don't let your happiness depend on one relationship, project, or job. Having lots of options to work towards takes the pressure off and increases your chances of success. And before you set things in motion, imagine the worst that could possibly happen and how you would cope. This takes away the fear of rejection; and if the worst does happen—which probably won't—you will know what to do.

3. Is there something that you have always wanted to do, someone you long to get to know, but fear of failure is holding you back? Don't sit and wait for the perfect moment. It doesn't exist. Pick up the phone, write that letter, send that application, start that diet, apply for that course right now. If it works out, great. If it doesn't work out, pat yourself on the

back for having had the courage to try.

4. Stress and tension often lead to inappropriate actions and words. The person you finally scream at often has nothing to do with the stress-inducing circumstances that created your anger. Before you reach the point of explosion, find a quiet and private spot. Stretch your mouth as wide as you can and tense your face, neck and head muscles. Then clench your fists and beat the air and scream. Then relax and do it again until you feel the tension leave you. It is important to let stress go quickly when life isn't going your way. Stress lowers your ability to change your life for the better.

5. Think about what attitude you are projecting. When you walk into a room, what image do you project? When you start a diet, do you expect to succeed? When you apply for a job, are you convinced you are the best person for it? Are you the one sabotaging your chances of success? If you project a sense of impending rejection, you'll almost certainly be rejected. What can you do to project a more positive image? Discover your inner film star. To get what you want you have to feel you deserve it. Go out and buy something lovely to wear, get a haircut that gives you a whole new look. When you dress and act like a film star, you often feel like one.

6. If something doesn't work out as planned, consider the possibilities with an open mind. Write down every approach you can think of that will lead to your goal. Find other ways to make it work. For example, if you aren't meeting potential partners through your work and friends, try a dating agency, join a club, or do an evening class in a subject that interests you and where you might meet like-minded people.

7. Are you endlessly thinking about what went wrong? Why not

take a break and start thinking about something else. Book a holiday, arrange to see friends, go shopping, mow the lawn, read a book. Tell yourself that thinking about the same thing over and over again isn't going to resolve anything. Keeping busy opens your mind to other thoughts, pushing the old ones aside. One thought generates others, and the next thing you know is that the space in your mind that was filled with disappointment is now filled with questions, challenges, and new dreams.

8. Spending your time imagining what might have been is counterproductive and leaves you unhappy. We can all look back and regret our actions, but we cannot change the past. Stop blaming yourself right now and let go of the past. Remember, you did the best you could at the time, and now you must look forward to a more positive future. Instead of thinking about what might never happen in the future, think about how you can improve your future.

9. Have you ever been upset by the rain, the sun, the temperature, or the fog? You cannot change the weather. Don't let yourself get stressed about something you cannot control. Forget about the weather. Go on and enjoy your life.

15

Push Your Luck

What you pay attention to, you get more of. It's a universal principle. When you turn your attention to how lucky you are, the luckier you will become. You may not win the lottery this week or ever win an Olympic gold medal, but focusing on the positive will make you feel happier—and happy people are, after all, the luckiest people in the world.

Keyword: Hope

The Luck Equation

Passion + focus + adaptability + charm + humility + generosity + insight + resilience + hope = good luck

The quality that motivates and inspires all the others is a strong belief in yourself and your abilities. The degree of success you have in life is greatly determined by your self-image. We looked at self-esteem earlier and we learned that those who have good self-esteem tend to attract more luck, whereas those with a low opinion of themselves attract only unhappiness and failure.

Lucky people don't think 'what if' and 'may be'. They think 'will' and 'when'. They look for opportunity in every setback, and they create a self-image that is so heroic that it serves as a protection when they encounter tough times.

ADJUST YOUR SELF-IMAGE

Your self-image guides your life in much the same way as an automatic pilot guides an aeroplane. Unless you can alter its course it will keep you going in the same direction. If your self-image is set for failure, it will fail. So how can you alter your course from failure to success?

Start with your conscious mind. Notice when you begin thinking of yourself as a loser. Replace those negative beliefs with more positive images of yourself. For example, every time you think 'I am stupid,' contradict this with something positive, like 'I am intelligent.'

Then work to change your self-image at a subconscious level. The most effective way to do this is to learn to use and control your imagination, a technique sometimes called visualisation.

JUST IMAGINE

Imagination is the key that will unlock the door to your success. You can't accomplish anything without it first being pictured in your mind. The way to success is to see yourself succeeding. The way to luck is to expect luck. Picture it first in your mind. Believe you can do something, and then go out and make it happen. Here's a fun exercise that may help you.

BE YOUR OWN HERO

> In your mind create an image of yourself like the heroes of one of your favourite adventure films. You face ups and downs, but in the end victory is yours. Think Harrison Ford or Julia Roberts. You battle life's negative forces but are always ready for a challenge, and you know you will triumph in the end, because you are determined to reach your goal at all costs. Imagine yourself ending up happy, rich, and lucky. Visualise a grand finale when you fight hard and win. The music begins, and you are a hero.

> The more vivid your images of success the more you will trick your mind into believing they are real and you are going to overcome setbacks and be lucky. Your mind will become activated, and opportunities that can help you, even in crisis, will appear. Whenever you face setbacks run this imaginary film in your mind and it will recharge your enthusiasm. You may feel a little silly doing this exercise, but it will have an impact on the way you think about luck. It will help you feel that happiness and luck are things you are entitled to.

You may ask, isn't visualisation just daydreaming or wishful thinking? No, it is a powerful technique to move you, not in the direction of your past habits but towards becoming the person you want to be. The hardest part is getting started. Don't expect miraculous results instantly. It will take a few weeks at least before you see any changes. The main thing is to replace negative thoughts about yourself with positive ones, over and over again. Repetition is important. Simply believe and persevere. You are sending data to your subconscious mind that will eventually become your bedrock truths.

As your new self-image grows you will find yourself becoming more confident and effective. You'll see yourself developing a feeling that nothing the world throws at you can shake you. Other people will begin to see in you what you see in yourself. They will react to you differently. You feel better, think better, look better, as you become the person you have always wished to be: the confident, successful person of your imagination. As you start to develop this winning side of your personality you begin to change your ideas about the uncertainty of luck. You begin to expect it.

Feel like a winner

How do you begin becoming that hero in your everyday life? Practise the feeling of being a winner. This winning feeling will overcome difficulties that otherwise might seem impossible. You've enjoyed the taste of success from time to time, even though they may have been small victories. Try to recall one of these and focus on it.

> The incident isn't as important as the feeling of success and satisfaction coming from it. It doesn't have to be a huge victory, like getting promoted or becoming a parent. Even a small one will do, like winning a game of darts or getting your Christmas shopping done on time. Try to recall a successful experience that happened to you. Fill your mental picture with all the details you can recall, and relive the feelings. As you relive them you will not only remember how you felt but will actually experience feelings of confidence and success.

What if your only experience is failure and you haven't got anything you want to focus on? The answer is, you create an experience. When you imagine something with vivid reality it becomes reality in your subconscious mind. If you don't have a backlog of successful experiences to draw on, create an imaginary one. Your subconscious mind won't be able to tell the difference.

> Now project this winning feeling onto the outer world of reality. Apply it to whatever objective you are striving for at the present time. Athletes often use this technique to improve their performance. They see themselves winning the race or the game. So in your mind's eye see yourself moving towards your goal with poise and confidence. Capture the mental attitude of winning. This state of mind will immediately fill you with a surge of exhilaration and vitality, propelling you towards your self-fulfilling prophecy of success.
>
> By pre-living this affirmation as a reality and conducting

> your thoughts throughout each day as if it were really true, you gradually incorporate it into your mind at both a conscious and an unconscious level. Practise this every day. Maintain a clear, detailed picture of your goal achieved, and the means of accomplishing it will often be supplied by the creative powers of your subconscious mind.

As you change your expectation of yourself and your luck, both you and your luck will start to improve. By improving your mind pictures you can dramatically change your luck for the better. Mind pictures are like magnets pulling you towards what you picture. So it is important to control what you picture. Choose your thoughts wisely. What you habitually visualise may very well become reality. There is only one person responsible for the way you think: you. You build your destiny thought by thought.

Faith

To have faith is to be sure of things we cannot see. We should expect luck in whatever situation we find ourselves—full of hope for the future. We would all like to believe our success in life is due to ourselves, but no matter how lucky we get we are never completely whole until we have a spiritual element in our lives. This can help us transcend the frailty of human nature and release our inner strength. Research[62] has shown that regardless of what religion people are affiliated to, those who had strongly held beliefs were typically satisfied with life, while those who had no faith were typically unsatisfied.

Maintain a sense of hope for the world. Studies[63] show that people who believe the world is ultimately just have a higher level of life satisfaction than those who do not. That there are many problems in the world is obvious, but have faith that the world is ultimately just. Believe that there is plenty of luck to go around. Expect it and it will change your life. Your abilities are important, to be sure, but believing you can succeed determines to a great extent whether you will or not. Faith is the most powerful force in the universe.

So believe in yourself, in your potential. Unwavering belief is the one absolutely essential element in lucky people. It generates the ability and the enthusiasm necessary to attract luck, to become a winner in life. Believe you can succeed, and you will.

Think big

There is not one person reading this book who is living up to their full potential. It is estimated that the average person uses less than 1 per cent of his or her potential. You have within you the ability to achieve far more than you realise. Rid yourself of the belief that you are born with or without something. Alter your self-limiting beliefs and improve your ability to excel.

Before 1954 everyone thought it was impossible to run a mile in less than four minutes. Then along came Roger Bannister, who didn't believe in barriers. He set a new world record. He broke through an attitude of self-limitation; and once he had smashed the world record, runners all over the world were recording four-minute miles. Why did this happen? Because a long-held belief had been shattered.

Of course there are limits to how much we can achieve, but the reason we do not achieve peak performance is because we don't realise what our limits really are. Running the four-minute mile is the same as achieving any other goal. It is our mental barriers that must be overcome first. If we strongly believe we can achieve something, we will.

Be realistic and use your common sense, but don't be satisfied with just getting by. Raise your luck potential and break your limitations. Visualise with anticipation the way you want to be, and your behaviour will catch up with the mental picture you have of yourself.

Expect good luck

Do you hope for good fortune, or do you expect it? People who are lucky believe with absolute certainty that they will have everything they need, even when life doesn't go according to plan. Bad luck is temporary, and things will turn out for the best. There will always be days when they doubt themselves, but they will always return to a quiet knowing that the world is a good place and their needs will be taken care of.

So, you may ask, what about the lottery winner who has been a pessimist all his or her life? Well, just the fact that he or she bought the ticket in the first place shows a degree of optimism. And lottery win or not, if that person doesn't have a positive attitude towards life, large sums of money will only make them more comfortable, not happier. If you aren't happy, you aren't really lucky at all.

We tend to get what we expect. People are about as lucky as they make up their minds to be. Expecting to be disappointed almost guarantees it. Expecting fulfilment makes you much more likely to find it. To create luck in your life you must not only wish for it, you must believe that it is possible and work towards making good luck happen. You must also fully expect to receive it, so that when it comes your way you are ready to accept it.

Start believing that you can be a lucky person. Expect luck even when you aren't really sure. Then you won't feel so uncertain any more and you will commit yourself to taking action that will draw it to you.

You are not unlucky

> 'Many of us have heard opportunity knocking at our door, but by the time we unhooked the chain, pushed back the bolt, turned two locks and shut off the burglar alarm it was gone.' (Anonymous)

Negative and pessimistic thinking can scare good luck away. We all have moments when a voice inside our head tells us we can't, we shouldn't, we'll never do it, or other people make us doubt ourselves. The secret is to catch these negative thoughts before they completely demotivate us.

To catch these negative thoughts, work out how they got there. Have a think about the roots of your pessimistic thoughts. What negative labels have you pinned on yourself and the world? What triggered your negative thinking? What are your thoughts about money and prosperity? Do you believe that people are fundamentally good or bad or that they have a choice? Were you criticised as a child? Did you grow up thinking the world is a kind, safe place? What do you think about luck in general? Do you deserve to be lucky? What are your superstitions about luck?

If you are expecting to be disappointed, perhaps you are using your expectation as a defence mechanism. If you expect to be let down, you won't be hurt or surprised. In a strange way you have control, because you predicted exactly what would happen. Also, when you think of yourself as unlucky, you don't have to take responsibility: it isn't your fault. You may even be proud of how you have survived bad luck. Yes, resilience is admirable, but good luck is better. This defence mechanism is keeping good luck away.

Have a good long think about how much you expect disappointment in your life. If the pattern has been embedded in you since childhood, you may need some hard work to turn it around. You have to be willing to give up the payoffs of being unlucky. Like learning a new language or moving to a new area, it will take effort to get there, but once you get the hang of it you will be so glad you put in the effort. You can get to work right now with a positive expectation that you can change your negative self-talk into positive self-talk. You might need professional help if you don't know where to start with this, but the following might help.

Every time you catch yourself saying 'I never' or 'I'm not,' change it to 'I seldom' or 'I often.' This will give you hope. Instead of 'I never make friends', say 'Until now I have not made friends.'

Think about all the pessimistic statements you make about yourself. I never win. Luck slips through my fingers. I'm a loser. Other people are luckier than me. Then think about alternative, luck-building statements. Someone has to win, why not me? If other people can be lucky, why not me? Luck does sometimes come my way. I can learn to make my own luck.

Every time you tell yourself you are unlucky, or always have bad luck, challenge it. Everything that happens to you, however disastrous, is a combination of experiences. Was everything about it unlucky? Was it all your fault? Could any good come out of it now or in the future? Am I being rational? Does this really matter?

If you really feel pessimistic and think it is unrealistic to change your opinion, try something like this. Instead of 'We will never be able to afford a house of our own' try 'As far as I know there is no way we can afford to buy a house of our own—unless something unexpected happens.' By adding the 'as far as I know' to your thoughts and ideas you remind yourself to expand your mind to include that which you do not know. You also open yourself to the possibility that circumstances could change, which they often do.

If other people are shoving negative opinions down your throat, try the same thing. For example, if your mother tells you that you'll never do anything with your life, imagine her saying, 'In my opinion you will never succeed.' Then you can remind yourself that her opinion is her point of view, and it's certainly not shared by everyone—least of all you. Things can always change for the better.

When a negative thought enters your mind, catch it

before it takes over, like weeds in a garden. Visualise yourself pulling out a negative thought weed, and then picture your garden returning to its natural beauty.

Think about how you can improve your future, but don't waste your present thinking about how you can change your past. Pondering past misfortunes endlessly won't get you anywhere. When you are driving and you take a wrong route, you don't ponder why you did that. You try to work out what to do next. Do the same in life, and start thinking about what you need to do to get from where you are now to where you want to be.

Many sad and terrible things happen in our world, but rather than focus on them, have hope for the future. Think of the world's potential, not the world's sorrow. Perhaps the curing of disease, the end of violence, poverty and hunger will happen one day. Research[64] shows that the difference between more and less happy people is what they do with their discomfort. Less happy people wallow in the problems they see, while happy people focus on potential improvements in the future.

One of our greatest sources of anxiety is the fear that we will never be able to do the things we want to do. Don't wait until the end of your life to work out what you wish you had done. Don't let fear of death panic you. Let it motivate you to think about what you really want to do. Research[65] on old people has shown that those who are the most comfortable with their own mortality do not ignore it but prepare for it. Think of the things you want to do, don't let *what if's* get in the way, and do them now.

Look for the silver lining

Research shows that lucky and unlucky people explain the world differently. Unlucky people tend to be quick to see the negative, whereas lucky people see the positive.[66]

There are three basic ways in which you can respond to bad luck. You can become a victim and a pessimist, like those people you don't want to ask how they are because you know they are going to tell you that everything in their life is horrible and none of it is their fault. They are intent on feeling sorry for themselves, and every conversation with them is a depressing experience. Or you could be like those people who see the blessing in adversity, but only with hindsight. When the unwelcome experience is happening, they grumble and moan and wish things could be different, but once the difficulties have passed they look back and discover that something positive did come from it. Most people fall into this category. The third group are those who look for blessings from the moment they experience adversity. Most of the time these are lucky people.

When you talk to these people you marvel at how strong and optimistic they are. You hear about their troubles, but you also hear about their hope and what they are doing to solve the problem. They will also probably ask you how you are doing. Unlike victims, they don't see the universe revolving around themselves. Scientists[67] have a hard time predicting one's happiness based on that person's experiences. A better predictor of happiness is the belief and attitude adopted by that person towards these events.

> Simon, aged twenty-six, is a joy to be around. His optimism and sense of humour delight everyone he comes into contact with. Simon was involved in a horrific accident. His motorcycle collided with a lorry at a roundabout. His bike went down, and the petrol can popped open. The petrol poured out and caught fire, and seventy per cent of his body was burned. Fortunately the quick-thinking lorry driver doused Simon with a fire extinguisher and saved his life. Even so, Simon's face was burned off, his fingers were twisted, and his legs were nothing but raw red flesh. He was unconscious for ten days. He had four months of operations

> and corrective surgery. It has taken him five years to learn to adjust to his handicaps. Despite all this, Simon is a sought-after speaker, a wheelchair athlete, and a writer. His secret is twofold. First of all the love and support of his family made him realise he did not have to buy society's notion that you have to be handsome and healthy to be happy. And secondly, he chooses to focus on what he has, not what he has lost. He sees his accident as a starting point, not an ending.

Although most of our setbacks won't be as debilitating as Simon's, we too need to be positive and strong. So right now if you are experiencing difficulties, don't wait until things resolve themselves to find the positive. Find the silver lining now. Sometimes life offers unbearable heartbreak, like the loss of a loved one, and it may take much time before we gain our balance. But when it comes to everyday difficulties, no matter how tough your day has been you can always find something you are grateful for: your health, the love of your friends and family, healthy children, good food, and so on. The next time you feel sorry for yourself, are angry with someone or really depressed, try to focus on what you already have to help you shift into a luck-building mode. In the words of Helen Keller, 'So much has been given to me. I have no time to ponder that which has been denied.'

Appreciating what you have will help turn your luck around. Adopt an attitude of gratitude and you'll be surprised how much good luck you find.

Hang out with happy people

To push your luck even further, seek the company of people who are happy. Researchers[68] have found that having a good attitude about those around you is one of the most important predictors of happiness. If you had a challenge ahead of you—whether you were trying to climb a mountain or to do something at work—what kind of people would you like to be surrounded by? People who told you you would fail, or people who give you reasons to succeed? Mix with people who lift you up, and steer clear of those who drag you down. Success attracts success, just as negativity attracts negativity. Mix with people you admire and you will feel inspired to create your own success, and, of course, your self-esteem will increase too.

AGE DOESN'T MATTER

You are never too young or too old to be lucky. Don't convince yourself or let other people convince you that age is a handicap. You are not too young to achieve greatness. Isaac Newton was only twenty-four when he discovered the law of universal gravitation. Neither are you too old to start being successful. Many famous people achieved their greatest success late in life, at an age when most people would feel their best years were behind them. Grandma Moses painted her first picture at the age of seventy-six. When she died twenty-five years later she had made a million dollars.

Surveys[69] show that age is simply unrelated to levels of personal happiness. Researchers[70] conducted a long-term study, interviewing subjects many times over thirty years. When asked when they had been the happiest in their lives, each time eight out of ten replied, 'Right now.' You are never too young or too old to get lucky—unless you think you are.

SMILE

A group called the American Association of Humor believes that one of the things too often missing from our lives is humour. The message is being heard by an increasing number of business consultants, who find that laughter makes a better employee. Businesses are having contests and 'dress-down' days. Why? Because shaking ourselves out of our routine increases productivity, creativity, and job satisfaction. Whether at work or at home, the therapy and humour group says happiness is a laughing matter. In studies[71] of hundreds of adults the ability to laugh was seen as a source of happiness. Those who enjoy humour are more likely to feel happy than those who are more serious-minded.

Push your luck

Hopefully after reading this book you will never attribute someone's luck to pure chance again. The next time you say to yourself, 'They are so lucky,' have a think about what they have done to create that luck. Remember, your happiness and good fortune are in your hands and in your thoughts.

Research[72] has proved time and again that happiness is not dependent on the sum of events but on what is made of those events. Your luck follows from the decisions you make, the priorities you develop, and the perspective through which you see things. You have been given life, and with it you—and not someone else—have the opportunity to define it. You write your own life script. No matter what life throws at you or what you are forced to cope with, you can make good or bad luck out of it. You can hope for luck or you can push your luck. The choice is yours.

It's a wrap

> A preacher finds himself caught in a tremendous rainstorm. Within a few hours the motel he's staying in is flooded. As the water rises, the preacher climbs onto the roof and starts praying.
>
> Just then, a rescue party floats by in a rowing boat. 'Let's go, mister: into the boat.'
>
> 'I'll stay here,' says the preacher. 'The Lord will save me.'
>
> An hour later a second boat reaches the motel. 'You better get in. The water is still rising.'
>
> 'No, thanks,' says the preacher. 'The Lord is my salvation.'
>
> Towards evening the motel is almost completely under water, and the preacher is clinging to the satellite dish on the roof. 'Hey, buddy, get in the boat! This is your last chance.'

> 'I'm all right,' says the preacher, looking towards Heaven. 'I know the Lord will provide.'
>
> As the boat departs, the satellite dish is hit by lightning, and the preacher is killed. When he arrives at the Pearly Gates he is furious. 'What happened?' he shouts. 'I thought the Lord would provide!'
>
> Within seconds a thunderous reply is heard: 'Gimme a break, pal. I sent three boats!'

Lucky people have an image of themselves—of what they want to become—and they practise daily. Losing is a habit, but so is winning. Winning habits are learned and retained; and losing habits, such as anxiety, fear, depression, dishonesty, greed, and insensitivity, are lost. Lucky people begin by fantasising their own life scripts as if their lives were a magnificent film and they are writer, producer, director, and star.

When you project the nine qualities of lucky people into your life, they become your nine commandments for personal growth and the achievement of your own individual definition of success. Don't be like the preacher and miss the boat. Make your own opportunities, and become the lucky person you deserve to be.

Actions to take today to push your luck

1. What are the negative mind traps that trip you up? Make a decision to replace them with positive alternatives. For example, replace devastation with disappointment, failure with setback, caution with courage, and making mistakes with missing opportunities. It's surprising how the words we use can affect how we see a situation. The Chinese character for crisis is also the character for opportunity. What a good way to see difficulties! Instead of becoming problems they become challenges and opportunities for us to grow and increase our power to change things.
2. As you go through your day, watch your 'buts'. Notice when

you put the emphasis on the negative. For example, 'My family has been great, but I feel terrible.' With practice you can say the same thing but keep a more optimistic outlook. Stress the positive and not the negative in your interpretation of events. Instead of mentioning the positive first and then discussing all the negatives about your day, switch things around. Talk about the negatives briefly first and then discuss all the positives. Save the good news for after your 'but'. 'I feel unwell, but my family have been great.' This shifts the emphasis to the positive. It shows what you are choosing to focus on and how much luck you bring into your life in the rebuilding process.

3. Write every day in a special notebook about all the things you are grateful for. It doesn't have to be mind-blowing stuff. The process of jotting things down on paper is a great way to refocus your mind. Try to include things for which you wouldn't normally be grateful. For example, if you get a parking fine, be grateful your car wasn't towed away; if you break something, be grateful that you didn't get injured, and so on. Be sure to include the silly stuff. It is okay to be grateful for Starbucks mocha with whipped cream!

4. Buy what you need. Don't buy things because you want a lot of stuff. On the other hand, don't deny yourself something you really want or need. The purpose of saving is to give you what you need. If there is something you really need and can afford but keep putting off, like a coat, a holiday, or a night out, go ahead and buy it.

5. Protect your positive feelings and self-esteem, and stay away from grumpy people who are always complaining and casting themselves in the role of victim. These people seem determined that they and you will never have a good day.

6. Develop a vibrant vision of your future. The more you think about the way you want your life to be, the more chance you

have of developing a plan that is going to bring you happiness. Having a powerful vision of what you want helps put the rest of your life in perspective. You can let your vision gently pull you towards the future of your dreams. Start by focusing specifically on the next three years. Imagine re-reading this book in three years' time. What has happened over those three years, both in your personal life and work life? How do you feel? Who are you as a person? What has happened to make you feel happy and pleased with your progress?

7. Look in the mirror and really smile with all your face—eyes as well as mouth. Look closely at your smile and see how it lights up your face. Practise your smile when others are around. The smiling habit helps you look outside yourself, and sometimes this is all you need to trigger a change in your feelings and to increase your self-esteem.

8. Find a comfortable place, close your eyes, and follow your breathing until you feel deeply relaxed. Then picture a scene where you look confident and relaxed. Feel what it is like to be a success. See people treating you with the respect you deserve. Make the vision real: create sound effects, notice the colours, feel your success. When you are ready let the scene melt away, open your eyes, and come back into the room.

9. The satisfied life[73] is not one of extremes but of steady, generally positive feelings. Many days will be ordinary days. You can't have highlights all the time. Yet within these regular days there are many opportunities for enjoyment, inspiration, and fulfilment. Be grateful for what you have achieved so far, and focus on what is good about your life right now. Gratitude and an optimistic attitude are prerequisites for a lucky, happy life. Squeeze them out of your present circumstances however you can. Make every day your lucky day.

PART THREE

Good Luck

When a lot of good luck comes together in your life something wonderful happens. Along with an abundance of opportunities you have a magical energy that other people find irresistible. They want to be around you. Who knows, they might catch some luck. Lottery winners, celebrities, sports heroes, successful gamblers and pop stars often tell stories of being touched by people hoping to catch some luck. This is what I have tried to do here. I want to wish you good luck, so I gathered lots of luck in one place. Hopefully you might catch some.

And because tradition tells us that good luck charms work best if they are found, given, or received as a gift, I hope you'll accept this hybrid selection of good luck charms, customs and beliefs as my parting gift to you. Good reading, and good luck.

16

The Power of Luck

Touch wood, human beings will probably believe they can influence luck until the end of time, as they have from the beginning. With all our charms, amulets and talismans, rituals, invocations and signs, we seem to have a certain faith beyond reason that we can win a smile from Lady Luck.

Many of us are superstitious without even knowing it. We knock on wood, step on cracks in a pavement, and would never walk under a ladder or open an umbrella in a house. You may have a lucky suit or hat or a lucky charm you wouldn't ever part with. And many people have their own lucky number, which is most likely to be an odd number, since odd numbers are thought to be luckier. Rabbits' feet, horseshoes and four-leaved clovers are among the most well-known good luck charms. And on the bad-luck side, American folklore has it that these results are to be expected if you ignorantly or foolishly do the following:

> Sneeze at table—poor health in the family
> Break a mirror—seven years' bad luck
> Kill a frog—a cow will die
> Count graves—bad luck
> Drop a book and don't step on it—worse luck

Do any of these beliefs work? Yes, sometimes they do. Why? Because, as I have stressed throughout this book, people believe they do. The mind exerts a tremendous influence over our lives. But surely in this enlightened age no-one still believes such things, do they?

It's quite amazing that in this day and age of scepticism and debunking, superstitions are still alive and well. We spend millions on methods based on superstitious beliefs, such as fortune-telling and good luck charms, that claim to improve our luck.

Remember to keep an open mind

Good luck charms and customs are a way of asking fate a favour. After reading this book you may scorn the idea. Charms can only bring luck because you expect that they will, and a positive attitude about luck attracts luck, right? While this is undoubtedly true, don't get so carried away that you lose all sense of humility. Remember, it doesn't hurt to keep an open mind.

Believing in luck is believing that life is a series of opportunities where things are never quite what they seem. That's why this section pays tribute to the enduring magic and mystery of luck. Time-honoured customs and beliefs can still teach us valuable lessons about ourselves and the nature of luck. What matters here is not whether these beliefs are right or wrong but the sense of wonder and positive expectancy you are left with. If anything you read here can reassure, intrigue, humble or inspire you, then you are truly opening your mind and the door to luck.

Luck is real—superstition isn't

Throughout the ages luck has been linked with superstition. In an effort to find ways to attract good fortune and protect ourselves from bad luck, a variety of superstitious beliefs have developed. From seeing a black cat to finding a coin or sneezing, we can see hidden meanings in the world all around us, if we choose to. There is nothing wrong with this, as long as you make sure you don't confuse superstition with luck itself. Superstition isn't real, but luck is. Luck is undeniable. Luck is out there waiting.

And don't let superstition become an excuse for not facing your own responsibility. There seem to be more beliefs about avoiding bad luck than there are about creating good luck. Is this because we like to think that when good luck happens it is due to our hard work or that we deserve it, whereas when something bad happens we don't like to blame ourselves? Remember that one of the quickest ways to change your luck for the worse is to avoid responsibility.

As long as you make a clear distinction between luck and superstition there is no harm in it. In fact finding meaning in the ordinary can help you attract luck, because you live in hope and expectancy of it and you start focusing your thoughts on what you want to achieve.

Beautiful and wonderful things can and do happen in our lives—sometimes for a reason and sometimes for no reason we can discern. Whatever you choose to believe, may all the beautiful and wonderful things you hope for yourself and others come true. And may all that you wish for come true too.

17

CHARMS

The word *charm* has its roots in the Latin word for song—not just any song but a song of enchantment, rather like that which a snake charmer uses. Another word for charm is an *amulet*—an object worn to protect the wearer against harm, bad luck, evil spirits, and enemies. Charm bracelets from ancient times comprised amulets that offered protection. The word *talisman* pretty much means the same thing. *Mascot* also means something that brings good luck. The concept has been around since the beginning of time, and it still survives today. Cats rode in Egyptian war chariots, and modern schoolchildren take cuddly toys into exam rooms.

Whatever you call them, charms, mascots, talismans, or amulets, they are thought to protect against evil and offer protection and good luck. By tradition most good luck charms work only if they are found or given or received as gifts. This doesn't mean you can't buy lucky charms for yourself. What tradition is trying to remind us is that luck cannot be bought: it can only be accepted gratefully. If you truly believe something can bring you good luck, you do in a way endow it with a magical power. In the words of Francis Bacon, 'charms have not their power from contacts with evil spirits but proceed wholly from strengthening the imagination.'

Listed alphabetically below are some well-known good luck charms and in the next chapter a selection of good luck customs and beliefs. It would be impossible to list them all, and this selection is by no means complete. There are as many good luck charms as there are people to believe in them.

CHESTNUTS

In many different countries horse-chestnuts are carried to bring good luck, good health, and long life. It is not clear why this should be, but it could be because chestnuts have a long life and therefore good health and good luck. But it is probably much more obvious than that. It is almost impossible not to pick up a chestnut when you see a scatter of them on the ground, and when you touch them they feel smooth and pleasant. Stroking them makes you feel comforted and connected with nature.

DARUMA DOLL

This is Japan's most common good luck charm. It is named after a sixth-century monk who, according to legend, sat so long in meditation that he lost his arms and legs. The Daruma doll looks like an egg-shaped person with a round bottom. When you knock the doll over, it pops back up again, and because it recovers time and time again it is a symbol of resilience, luck, and success. The Japanese buy a Daruma before starting something new. It comes with both eyes painted white, with no pupils. You paint in one eye to make a wish, and if the wish comes true you paint in the other eye for thanks.

FAIRY STONES

It is hard to resist picking up pebbles on a beach, and a strange-looking stone kept from a pleasurable day out is one of the oldest lucky charms. But Virginia Cross fairy stones are some of the strangest-looking stones you could possibly find. They are dark brown or whitish and about an inch or two long, formed in the shape of tiny crosses, the cross being a widespread symbol of hope and compassion. Thousands of people around the world carry fairy stones as amulets against misfortune and danger. The legend associated with the stones is beautiful. It is believed that fairies once danced through the mountain glades of the Blue Ridge. When the fairies heard news from an elfin messenger that Christ had been crucified they cried, and the mountain was strewn with their crystalline tears, which fell to earth in the shape of tiny crosses.

Four-leaf clover

Four-leaf clovers are thought to be lucky throughout Europe and North America. People once believed that the person who found a four-leaf clover would be granted special powers to see unseen evil spirits who can cause mischief. Christians say that the four leaves represent the cross. Another tradition says that Eve stopped to retrieve a four-leaf clover as she and Adam were driven out of the Garden of Eden, and she kept it as a memento of paradise lost. Such a clover, therefore, brings the fortunate finder a portion of paradise. Mediaeval Christians believed that the plant protected them against witchcraft, and folk medicine in those times used the four-leaf clover's presumed powers to purify the blood and heal sores. Its value as a charm once depended on its rarity—it's a mutation on the normal three-lobed variety—but nowadays the four-leaf clover is not so rare, as since the 1950s it is possible to produce them in a laboratory. If you do find a four-leaf clover growing naturally—a leaf for fame, a leaf for wealth, a leaf for love, and a leaf for health—keep it. Don't give it away, or you'll bring bad luck on yourself.

Horseshoe

Horseshoes nailed above someone's door for luck (with the points facing up so the luck doesn't spill out) are very common in many countries. 'That the horseshoe may never be pulled from your threshold' is a common way to wish someone well in England. It is best if you are given the horseshoe rather than buying it for yourself. You shouldn't pull out any of the nails, as you'll keep your luck for as many years as there are nails. The more nails the horseshoe contains, the luckier it is presumed to be.

From the air Stonehenge looks like a horseshoe, so the ancient people may have found mystic significance in the horseshoe too. But why is the horseshoe so lucky? Because it combines three things that for centuries have been associated with luck: horses, iron, and the crescent shape.

Horses have long been worshipped as magical animals, and any part of them is linked to good fortune—except in China, where the horseshoe isn't considered lucky but the hooves are. Iron has been considered lucky since ancient times. When people learned to fashion weapons from it, they discovered it to be very effective in hunting and battle. It's not hard to see why they associated iron with protective magic. All over the world iron is a charm against ghosts, witches, and evil spirits. Anything made of iron can be seen as a protection. Irish people, we are told, once belived that nothing bad can happen to a blacksmith. Moreover, the iron horseshoe can be worked on by heating with fire, and several early philosophers considered fire a purifying element, spiritually as well as literally. But perhaps the most powerful symbol of all is the crescent shape of the horseshoe. Horseshoes resemble the horned new moon, which is a symbol of life-creating force of great mother figures, like the Egyptian goddess Isis and the Greek goddess Artemis. Nailing a horseshoe above the door is a way of fighting the forces of death with the forces of life.

JADE

China is the place you think of as having the greatest reverence for jade as a good luck charm, but jade has been treasured in cultures all over the world. It is easy to understand the fascination with jade, for it is a beautiful stone, when polished, and can range in colour from green to white, yellow, orange, or black—although the green stone is considered the luckiest. It is quite rare, extremely hard, and virtually impossible to scratch. It is also cool to touch, and this gives it a soothing, mysterious quality.

Leprechauns

A popular good luck charm in Ireland is a tiny elfin shoemaker carrying a hammer. According to legend the leprechauns found pots of gold left by the Danes when they marauded Ireland and buried them. The leprechaun must give his treasure to whoever sees him, but you have to be clever and quick-witted, as the little leprechaun is a sly fellow who will try to trick you into turning away as he escapes into the forest.

As long as there are people who believe in the wee folk there will be leprechauns to reflect the well-known Irish sense of hospitality, wit, and fun. The Irish have a strong connection with luck. People use the phrase 'the luck of the Irish' when a person of Irish descent inexplicably beats the odds. It probably derives from the idea that because the Irish have suffered so many misfortunes, it's a miracle whenever something comes out right for them, and it can only be explained by being blessed with an inherited form of good luck.

Loadstone

Since ancient times magnetic iron ore, a naturally occurring black stone, has been used as a good luck charm. It was thought that these amazing stones could attract not only iron but all sorts of good things. In the East Indies they were thought to attract power and good fortune. Another magical idea that became associated with loadstones is that they could help people get lucky in love, because the way loadstone attracts iron is similar to the way two lovers are attracted to each other. In China it is known as the loving stone, and there is an old Spanish belief that if a lover wishes a woman to fall in love with him, all he needs to do is grind a little loadstone and swallow it before going to bed, and she will be magnetically drawn to him. The loadstone is also thought to help soothe strife and discord between a man and a woman, and is considered a remedy against wounds, snake bites, headaches, and poor hearing. So if you are fortunate enough to be given a loadstone, how can you have bad luck?

Rabbit's foot

Rabbits are fertile, as fast as lightning, and clever too: they often outwit the best hunters. Small wonder, then, that the rabbit has assumed magical properties.

In ancient times magic was thought to be contagious. Part of an object possesses the properties of the whole, even if contact is severed; and since a rabbit's hind legs gave it speed, it was used as a good luck charm. The rabbit's foot evolved into a talisman with healing powers. Rabbits were thought to have the power to ward off the evil eye, a belief that stemmed from the erroneous notion that they were born with their eyes open. The animal's burrowing habit contributed to its charmed reputation, because in ancient times people feared what might lie beneath the earth, and they naturally thought the rabbit must have mysterious power over darkness and evil there. In modern times popular fiction has endowed the rabbit with cunning and wit. From Beatrix Potter's *The Tales of Peter Rabbit* to Richard Adams's *Watership Down*, the image of the invincible rabbit persists. Perhaps any animal that can maintain a good image for so long must indeed bring good luck. Today the rabbit's foot is sought after as a charm conferring good luck in general. Their popularity may have waned, but they are still sold as key-chains.

Scarab beetles

The scarab has been an amulet that offers protective powers for several thousand years. The scarab is a Mediterranean beetle, oval in shape like the stones of a scarab armband. The ancient Egyptians compared the scarab's habit of laying a single egg and rolling it in dung to a hatching place, to god rolling the sun across the sky, giving life to earth. The scarab became an amulet signifying life and fertility, and by the fourth century the Phoenicians were producing scarab bracelets for sale throughout the Mediterranean.

Turquoise

Since ancient times turquoise has been considered a lucky stone that can bestow health. Reverence for the lucky sea-blue stone dates from the early dynasties of Ancient Egypt. There is an old tradition that if your health is poor, the turquoise ring or necklace will grow pale in colour. Among the Pima people of southern Arizona the luck-bestowing powers of turquoise were valued so highly that if someone lost a stone it was viewed as such an ominous sign that the medicine man would have to be called in to restore the lost luck.

Weefah

The weefah is an ancient Chinese good luck charm with five bats in a circle representing the five sources of happiness in life: luck, wealth, long life, health, and peace. The Chinese, who are always gracious about giving and receiving good luck, use the weefah to do just that. If you were a dinner guest at someone's house, you might empty your plate and find the weefah printed on the bottom.

18

Customs and Beliefs

Abracadabra

The word is thought to derive from the old Hebrew, meaning 'speak' or 'pronounce a blessing'. It is an incantation that dates back thousands of years. It was thought to cure fevers and bring good luck, provided it was written in a certain way:

abracadabr**a**
abracadab**r**
abracada**b**
abracad**a**
abraca**d**
abrac**a**
abra**c**
abr**a**
ab**r**
a**b**
a

As late as 1665 *abracadabra*, written in this form on linen and tied around the neck, was used to combat an outbreak of plague in England.

Today *abracadabra* has been relegated to the world of children's stories. But within that world it remains a powerful force. It fires the imagination and by so doing plays its part in creating our world.

CARDS

Blow on the cards. Sit on a square handkerchief. Ask for a new pack. Circle the table three times from left to right. Turn your chair around three times. Turn the back of your chair to the table and straddle it. Cross out your opponent's luck by putting matchsticks in a cross on the table. All this may or may not improve your luck, but it will make you feel less nervous. You need all your wits about you if you want to win at cards.

CHAIN LETTERS

Lucky chain letters, also known as chain-of-luck letters, have circulated for generations. People who continue the chain are promised good luck, and those who break the chain are promised bad luck. Many people decide not to tempt fate by not sending the letter on to someone we know. These letters when passed in multiple copies do show how quickly we can make connections with people around the world. And isn't that what luck is all about? The more connections you make in life, the greater the chance that at least one of these connections will lead to luck.

CREATURES WHO BRING LUCK

Many creatures around the world have been associated with luck since ancient times, teaching respect and admiration for all living things. We've mentioned horses and rabbits already, and here are some other well-known beliefs:

- There is an old idea that to have a cricket chirping in your house means good luck and to kill it means bad luck (like killing a ladybird or a spider). In Japan people have kept crickets inside their houses in tiny bamboo cages as a kind of good luck charm since the tenth century. Because a cricket chirps louder when rain is coming, it was valued as a weather forecaster. The Irish are said to believe that crickets are enchanted people hundreds of years old, and that if you could understand them they could tell you the history of the world. Today crickets are associated with fun, hospitality, and, of course, luck.

- Elephants are considered lucky because they are wonderful animals renowned for their memory, intelligence, strength, and longevity. In the Hindu religion the elephant god, Ganesha, is said to be a bringer of good luck, because he removes obstacles. His lucky image is often seen at the entrance of houses in India.

- If a strange dog follows you, good luck is just around the corner; but the dog that has been associated with luck for thousands of years is the Tibetan terrier. Highly valued by the Tibetans for their intelligence and devotion, they were never sold, for to do so would sell away their owner's good fortune. The first time one of these intelligent and faithful dogs left Tibet was in the early 1920s, when a grateful Tibetan nobleman gave one to a British doctor who cured his wife. Now they are kept as devoted pets all over the world.

- If a black cat walks across your path you have bad luck in store. This is a well-known belief, probably dating from the Middle Ages, when people thought witches could change into black cats. But black cats have also been associated with good fortune. In ancient Egypt people worshipped a fertile goddess named Bast, who was often depicted as having the head of a cat. The cats kept in temples were often considered gods themselves. Even domestic felines were loved, and their deaths were mourned as deeply as the passing of humans. The animals were sometimes embalmed and placed in valuable mummy cases.

  It is thought that if a stray black cat walks into your house, this is good luck, and fishermen's wives like to keep black cats to ensure the safety of their husbands at sea. King Charles I of England kept a black cat, and the day his cat died he said his luck was gone. Sure enough, he was arrested the next day.

In Japan the little statue of a kitten, a maneki-neko, waves its paw from the door of restaurants and businesses to lure customers.

- If a swallow builds a nest on your house it is thought that luck will visit your household.

- If a frog enters your house or garden you should be thankful: good luck comes with it. And on seeing the first frog of spring, make a wish and it will come true. Toads, on the other hand, are usually bad luck, although Gypsies believe that a tame toad is good luck.

- If you see three butterflies fluttering together, good luck is sure to be yours.

- Ladybirds are always a sign of good luck, especially if they land on you. Try to count the spots; each represents twenty-eight days of good luck. When it flies off, watch the direction it flies. This is where your good luck will come from.

- Find your initials in a spider's web and have good luck for ever. Spiders are thought to bring you good luck. In folklore spiders are wise and helpful. They are also persistent. But most of all, they are a symbol of prosperity. Perhaps there is a connection between a spider catching its prey and you catching money or business. Small spiders are called money-makers or money-spinners in England, and if one drops down in front of you, money will be coming your way. In Europe spider amulets are thought to help the wearer catch money. If a spider runs across your clothing, you will be getting new clothing. Keep one in your pocket and it will never be empty of cash. And it is bad luck to kill a spider. 'If you wish to live and thrive, let the spider run alive.'

- In many cultures around the world luck is associated with white animals, especially cows, hens, rabbits, elephants, horses, owls, butterflies, deer, and buffalo, white being a symbol of purity, innocence, and devotion.

THE EVIL EYE

Belief in the evil eye is one of the most widespread superstitions in the world Many good luck charms are meant to offer protection against it. Some anthropologists speculate that the fear arose in prehistoric times among people who cowered at the gaze of wild animals, human enemies, or jealous gods. Signs of the evil eye occur in artefacts of civilisations dating back four thousand years. Even today anthropologists encounter this belief among many peoples.

The evil eye is blamed for many misfortunes, ranging from crop failures to death. Prime targets are generally people and things that excite envy: beautiful women, healthy children, livestock that represents wealth. Folklore has it that presumed possessors of the evil eye, however, are not necessarily malicious, as the malignant power may be exerted consciously or unconsciously. Some people are merely carriers.

In Italy such carriers are called *jettafore*, and their ranks have included the famous and powerful. Various popes, Lord Byron and Napoléon III were all thought to be carriers. The Italian dictator Benito Mussolini was greatly fearful of the eye's power and would touch iron to ward it off—one of many defences known to believers. Charms and amulets of hunchbacks and blue ceramic beads painted to look like eyes have always been considered popular defences against the evil eye. A simple string around the wrist is thought by some to tie the soul to the body and thus thwart the eye. Ancient Egyptians applied make-up to ward off malevolent power, drawing dark circles around their eyes with kohl, and it is possible that the red dot worn on the foreheads of Hindu women is for the same purpose. Saliva is also an enduring antidote, with mediaeval nurses licking the faces of their children; and today, in some cultures, some mothers still spit on the faces of their children who they think may have been exposed.

The whole idea seems to have come from the fear that bragging too much or being too beautiful will attract the envy of evil spirits who want to take your good luck away from you. That is why we knock on wood after saying how well things are going. That is why a Hindu mother will say her child is unhealthy when it isn't, because to lavish praise might bring bad luck. Once again ancient traditions contain some deep, useful human wisdom about checking our pride and retaining our humility in the face of good fortune.

LUCKY FINDS

To find any of the following is thought to bring good luck: a postage stamp, a coin, a button, a pin, a horseshoe, a clean napkin, a four-leaf clover, a pencil, a yellow ribbon, and anything purple. Make sure you pick it up, because if you don't your luck will pass on to the person who does. It was especially lucky in former times to find a penny with the head side up.

FINGERS CROSSED

Keeping our fingers crossed is an expression used when someone is about to start something new. 'Keep your fingers crossed for me' is like saying 'Wish me luck!' Children cross their fingers while lying to cross out the lie, which comes from the belief that if you cross your fingers while lying, the Devil can't come and take you. People also cross their fingers when passing graveyards as a protection against evil spirits. One possible explanation is that the cross is used as a symbol of good, and where two straight lines meet our hopes are held there until they become reality. Crossing fingers, like crossing your legs—another time-honoured way to improve your luck—is self-protective. We are trying to cross out the possibility of bad luck and stop evil spirits changing our fortunes for the worse. It is a sign of humility, or, in the case of lying, an awareness of doing wrong.

Heirlooms

By tradition, as long as the family heirlooms are preserved it is thought that the family and fortunes are safe and sound. In the late Middle Ages, when nobles could not read, they would give a sword or a goblet as a symbol of their estates. The possession of a family's land and castle depended on that object. In the sixteenth century such objects became a cult, and by the eighteenth century many aristocratic families of England had something—a sword, a banner, a goblet—upon which they thought the well-being of the house depended. The cup of the family of Eden Hall is one of the most famous lucky heirlooms. Today the tradition of family heirlooms as good luck charms encourages a respect for past generations and the importance of family traditions.

Housewarming customs

To bring good luck into a house you must go into every room with a loaf of bread and a plate of salt. The best days for moving into a new house are Monday and Wednesday. The worst day is Friday. And always make sure you buy a new broom for your house. It is bad luck to move a broom from house to house.

Housewarming customs are not as daft as they might first appear. They are all concerned with making a clean break with the past and starting your life in a new place in a positive, expectant frame of mind. Housewarming presents are thought to bring good luck into a new household. It doesn't really matter whether they do or not: present-giving is always a great idea.

Ladder

Walking under a ladder may not be a wise move, in case something falls on you, but the ladder's reputation as an enemy of fortune far surpasses the logical reason. Some researchers believe that the ladder violates a taboo still observed in some societies among the people of south-east Asia that holding something above one's head diminishes them. Others relate the superstition to the number 3—symbolic of a divine trinity—and the fact that a standing ladder forms a triangle (a three-sided figure) against the wall. Piercing the triangle violates its integrity and invokes the wrath of the gods. There is good news, however, for the evil effects can be undone by making a wish, crossing your fingers until you encounter a dog, or spitting three times through the ladder's rungs.

Lay shee

The Chinese New Year is a time when everybody calls on friends and family to exchange good luck. Tea and sweets are offered to each guest, and in return the guest will give a little present of silver coins wrapped in red paper. This package is known as lay shee or 'good luck piece'. Red is a lucky colour in China; its symbolism goes back to blood and flame, the sources of life. Married and older people give lay shee to children and unmarried people, but it is in a way a luck exchange. In return for giving luck, they believe the vitality of the young people will help them.

Lucky looks

More often than not good luck is associated with a look or appearance that isn't conventionally considered attractive. This is significant. It teaches us that beauty isn't always the blessing it seems, and there is more to a person than meets the eye.

In Northumberland there is a tradition that if you are born with a gap between your front teeth you'll be lucky and will travel. In the English Midlands people with lots of body hair are born to be rich, and if you have webbed toes you will have luck all your life. White specks on your fingernails are said to mean good fortune, especially in money matters. In Japan good luck is associated with big ears. The seven gods of luck are often depicted with large, droopy ears, and Buddha statues also have enormous ears. (Rubbing Buddha's belly is thought to bring luck too.)

If you want to improve your finances choose an accountant or stockbroker whose eyebrows meet in the middle: this is supposed to be a good-luck sign for all matters to do with money. And if one of your eyelashes drops out and you find it, you have a chance to make a wish come true. Place it on the back of your left hand, then smack your left hand, from underneath on the palm with the back of your right hand. If it flies off by the third try it has gone to bring you good luck.

As far as clothing is concerned, wear something blue. Wearing blue is thought to improve your luck. The colour blue is considered to be lucky. It goes back to the idea that God lives in Heaven and Heaven is blue, and evil spirits are repelled by the colour blue. Brides are advised to wear something blue, of course, for luck—representing their respect and faith in their groom.

If you get up in the morning and put something on inside out by mistake, you have to wear it all day to make sure bad luck doesn't strike. This may or may not be so, but if you do spend a day feeling self-conscious because you are wearing something inside out, you are unlikely to make the same mistake again! You will have good luck if a friend or loved one gives you a button. If you are given a lot of buttons as gifts, you can make a bracelet out of them. As long as you wear your button bracelet your friendships cannot be ended. And, finally, to wear a ring on your thumb is thought to bring good luck, and changing the rings on your finger will change your luck.

LUCKY NUMBERS

When asked to select a number between one and ten, more

people will chose an odd than an even number. This is because odd numbers are generally thought to be luckier. According to Virgil in his eighth Eclogue, 'God delights in odd numbers.' The world was created in seven days. But in China the number 8 is a very lucky number.

> According to Zolar's *Encyclopaedia of Omens* the luckiest days of the year are:
> 4, 19, 27, 31 January
> 7, 8, 18 February
> 3, 9, 12, 14, 16 March
> 5, 27 April
> 1, 2, 4, 6, 9, 14 May
> 3, 5, 7, 9, 12, 23 June
> 2, 6, 10, 23, 30 July
> 5, 7, 10, 14, 19 August
> 6, 10, 15, 18, 30 September
> 13, 16, 20, 31 October
> 3, 13, 23, 30 November
> 10, 20, 29 December

THREE TIMES LUCKY

The number 3 has been considered a lucky number for centuries. Though the numbers 9 and 7 are also considered lucky, none has been more universally revered than 3. That's why so many lucky rituals are supposed to be repeated three times.

The sixth-century Greek philosopher Pythagoras described 3 as the perfect number. The triangle, with its three sides, was the most stable geometrical shape and considered a magic symbol that even had power to repel the devil. In Christianity, 3 represents the Trinity, and in pagan religions the moon has three phases: waxing, waning, and full. In China the third day of a new moon is thought to be lucky. A human being has body, soul, and mind. There is past, present, and future; animal, vegetable, and mineral; three cheers; three kisses on the cheek; three wishes.

LUCKY SEVEN

Seven has always been a significant number. The lunar cycle is twenty-eight days, a new phase beginning every seven days. In a week there are seven days, there are seven deadly sins, and there are seven wonders of the world. To the Ancient Greeks 7 was a perfect number. It is the sum of 3 and 4, the triangle and the square, which are regarded as two perfect figures. The number 7 is also significant for the Jewish religion, for Arabs, and for Hindus. One favourite theme of Japanese folklore is the seven gods of luck, who are whimsical deities associated with happiness and good fortune. It is thought to be good luck to have seven letters in your first or last name.

> If the date of your birth can be added up and then divided by 7—say 5/8/64 (5 + 8 + 64 = 77)—you will have good luck all your life.

THIRTEEN

The ancient Greeks dreaded the number 13. Some scholars believe it is because the mathematician and mystic Pythagoras declared that the number 12 embodied perfection. Going one number more was therefore imperfect—even evil. Others believe that it's because women have thirteen menstrual cycles a year, suggesting fear of women or the mysterious power of life. The mistrust of the number still exists today. Hotels frequently skip the thirteenth floor, and many airlines delete the thirteenth row of seats from their planes. Thirteen is considered an unlucky number for a dinner party.

When you put together the day of the crucifixion and the combined number of Christ and the apostles, including Judas, you get Friday and 13. Many people regard Friday the thirteenth with superstitious discomfort. But the number 13 hasn't always been thought of as unlucky. There is an old belief that children born on the thirteenth will be lucky in life. The Aztecs thought 13 had a mystical significance and built thirteen steps up to their platform of sacred fires; and even modern Judaism gives the number 13 special significance. The young United States showed no fear of the jinx. On the great seal of the United States there are thirteen stars, thirteen stripes, an eagle with thirteen features in each wing and the tail. It holds in one claw thirteen arrows and in the other a laurel branch with thirteen leaves and thirteen berries; there are thirteen letters in the mottoes beneath and thirteen clouds in the glory above.

The historian Ripley once constructed a list for Friday the thirteenth to show how lucky a date it was in American history. The thirteenth of the month actually falls on a Friday more than any other day. Over a period of four hundred years there will be 688 Friday the 13ths. Of Sundays and Wednesdays, the next most numerous 13th, there will be 687.

Pennies

There is a great deal of respect for this small unit of money. A penny minted during a leap year is thought to bring good luck in financial matters and should be kept as a lucky charm. The same is true for the first new coin that comes into your possession after the new year. If you mark a penny and it comes back to you, you will inherit money. It is a good idea to carry a little money in your pocket, as money attracts money. You will have good luck all week if you get pennies in change on a Monday; and if you get one with your date of birth on it keep it for extra luck. Finding any kind of money is undoubtedly lucky, especially if it has your date of birth on it.

The ancient custom of throwing pennies or coins into a fountain for good luck comes from the belief that spirits live at the bottom of fountains and demand that you pay homage. Giving lucky pennies goes back to the ancient practice of giving luck money after a purchase. In rural areas of Europe the seller of an animal always remembered to give some part of the purchase price back to the buyer, even if it was just a penny. This luck money would ensure the animal's health, so the business would not go sour. There is a lesson here. A small act of generosity can bring back more than you gave away.

AT RAINBOW'S END

Even though rainbows don't actually touch the earth, the myth that there is a pot of gold at the end is well known. But it is thought to be lucky even to see a rainbow. Take care not to point at it, though, as this may bring bad luck. A vivid rainbow is a beautiful thing; gazing at one, you cannot help but feel uplifted. In various cultures rainbows have been thought to be snakes, or spirits, but most often a soul bridge to heaven. In the Bible the rainbow is a sign of hope, and in a sense the rainbow is a good-luck charm. It tells us that the storm is over.

RIGHT TO LEFT

It is a very ancient idea that the right side is associated with good luck and the left side with bad. According to ancient beliefs, if your right ear or eye tingles it is a lucky omen, meaning that someone is speaking about you positively. If your right palm itches, money will come your way. The Romans feared that someone who entered a place with the left foot first would bring bad luck. Wealthy families used to employ footmen to ensure that every visitor 'got off on the right foot.'

If you do trip at an entrance or put your left foot first, go back and enter again. If you get up on the left (wrong) side of the bed, put on your right sock and shoe first. Passing to the left at a dinner table is good luck; passing to the right is bad luck. Performing a task from left to right puts you in sync with the sun's rhythm and its life-giving power. Today getting off on the right foot isn't taken literally, but the superstition reminds us how important it is to make a good impression and start with the best of intentions.

Salt

Because it preserves meat and other foods from decay, salt was and is of vital importance. Not surprisingly, it took on magical qualities associated with immortality and preservation. It became a part of many sacred rituals, especially those that have to do with making oaths or pledges. 'There is salt between us' is an old expression that means we are friends. Salt is also associated with keeping evil spirits at bay. That is why if you spill salt you must throw a pinch over your left shoulder, because left is associated with evil and bad luck. Old stories hold that salt tossed in such a way strikes the Devil in the eye and prevents him or her from doing any harm.

Sneezing

Sneezing was thought to bring good luck since ancient times, especially if you sneezed three times. To the ancients the violent expulsion of breath was a mystifying phenomenon, and in some cultures today it still is. To the Maori of New Zealand a sneeze is a sign of godlike power, as they believe that the creator sneezed life into the first human. The Zulu of southern Africa regard sneezing as the sign of a beneficent spirit. On the other hand, there is also a widespread notion that sneezing is unlucky, because it expels breath. Breath is equated with the soul, and to lose it is to die. Sometimes associated with this notion is the belief that sneezing made room for demons to rush in and possess the sneezer.

These beliefs are not as ridiculous as they seem. Death does involve a cessation of breath, and sneezing can denote illness; an obvious connection that was not lost on the ancients. Whether taken as a good or bad sign, sneezes always merit a response. The usual Greek response is to utter a brief blessing on the sneezer. Later the Romans were apt to say, 'May Jupiter be with you.' A heartfelt 'God bless you' became institutionalised in sixteenth-century Italy, when a sneeze might to be a precursor of plague.

Today when we say, 'Bless you,' it is simply saying take care of yourself.

Lucky star

'God made the heavens and luck made the stars' is an old Broadway saying. From the ancient idea that stars guide our destinies comes the idea of a guiding star for each person, which appears at our birth and disappears at our demise. It wanes and waxes, rises and falls, directing our life. Falling stars are especially lucky for lovers, provided they wish when they see one, and shooting stars are lucky for sick people. And if you can say 'money' three times before it vanishes you'll be prosperous. Today saying that you have a lucky star is a way of showing that you have humility and acknowledging how much you have to be grateful for in your life.

Wedding customs

There are many customs surrounding weddings. Many of the reasons behind them have been lost, but the intention is the same: to make sure the bride and groom have a wonderful day and a life together filled with love and happiness.

> June is the luckiest month for weddings, because Juno, the devoted wife of Jupiter in Roman mythology, blessed weddings held in that month. It is considered unlucky to let a friend try on your engagement ring, and it is also unlucky to wear it before you are engaged. It is luckier to have a new engagement ring than one worn by someone else. Wedding rings should be worn on the fourth finger of the left hand, because of the belief that there is a love vein that runs from the heart to that finger and the ring prevents the sentiments from escaping. It is considered lucky to have an even number of guests at the wedding and unlucky to have an odd number. A bride should wear something old from a

happily married person, because some of their luck may rub off, and something new to signify new beginnings. The something borrowed should be gold, which represents the sun, the source of life, and the colour blue signifies respect and faith. Bridesmaids should dress similarly to the bride in order to confuse evil spirits. The bride should be the first to cut the cake, and the groom should hold her hand as she does it to show that he wants to share in the good fortune. Then the wedding guests take some cake (luck) home with them. Rice is thrown at the bride and groom as a fertility symbol. There once was a time when a bride and groom really did tie a knot or a cord in the ceremony to keep good wishes from escaping. The word *honeymoon* derives from the Teutonic custom of drinking mead for twenty-eight days after the wedding. The bride is carried over the threshold in order to prevent her being tripped by evil spirits. There is nothing evil spirits hate more than happiness, love, and laughter, and they will do their best to spoil it.

Today all these customs ensure that a wedding ceremony has two essential ingredients: a sense of ritual to underline the significance of the union, and a sense of mystery to show that the love, happiness and laughter expected at the wedding should never be taken for granted.

Wishbone

We have all done it. We clasp one end of a dried turkey clavicle, with someone holding the other, and pull. Whoever gets the longer piece will have good luck and a wish come true.

This ritual dates from the third century, when hens were sacrificed to the gods. To the ancients, hens were steeped in magical power. The bird's forked breastbone was considered especially lucky because it resembled a pair of spread legs, symbolising fertility. If you do get the bigger piece of bone when you pull on a wishbone, you have got your lucky break.

This is one of those ancient customs that offer a great opportunity to focus your thoughts on the future. What better time to do that than after a good meal with a person you feel relaxed enough to break bones with!

Touch Wood

The custom of touching or knocking wood for luck probably comes from our tree-worshipping ancestors. In almost every culture trees have been worshipped either as gods themselves or dwelling places for spirits or gods who could exert power over our lives.

Touching wood today can still bring us good luck, because when we acknowledge that we are not all-powerful and good luck plays a part, we show our humility. To imply otherwise would appear arrogant and would incite envy and resentment in our listeners—not a good move.

Other Time-Honoured Ways to Improve Your Luck or Change Bad Luck to Good

★ Catch a falling leaf and keep it
★ Look at the new moon holding silver spoons in your hand
★ Tie a string in a circle and put it in your purse
★ Catch bubbles from your coffee or tea with a spoon and drink them before they break
★ Hide a lucky bean, and don't let anyone know where it is
★ Trim your fingernails on Monday morning before breakfast
★ Sprinkle nutmeg on your lottery tickets
★ Give a poor person a new pair of shoes
★ Before sleep, place your shoes with the toes pointing under the bed
★ If you break a mirror, wash a piece in a south-running river

To change bad luck to good pull a pocket inside out, walk up a flight of stairs backwards, or turn around three times: 'I turn myself three times about, and thus I put my bad luck to rout.'

'The only thing I have to worry about is bad luck. I never have bad luck.' (Harry S. Truman)

I hope one day you can say this to yourself!

Notes

1. R. Garrett, 'Wisdom as the key to a better world,' *Contemporary Issues in Behavior Therapy,* New York: Plenum 1996.

2. F. Clark et al., 'Life domains and adaptive strategies of a group of low income well older adults,' *American Journal of Occupational Therapy,* vol. 50 (1996), 99.

3. M. Minetti, 'Women's Educational Pursuits: Effects on Marital and Relationship Happiness' (master's dissertation, University of Nevada, Las Vegas, 1997).

4. E. Scope, 'A Meta-Analysis of Research on Creativity' (PhD thesis, Fordham University, New York, 1999).

5. P. Wu, 'Goal Structures of Materialists v. Non-Materialists' (PhD thesis, University of Michigan, Ann Arbor, 1998).

6. L. Jeffres and J. Dobos, 'Separating people's satisfaction with life and public perceptions of the quality of life in the environment,' *Social Indicators Research,* vol. 34 (1995), 181.

7. M. Sherer, 'The impact of using personal computers on the lives of nursing home residents,' *Physical and Occupational Therapy in Geriatrics,* vol. 14 (1996), 665.

8. H. Bless et al., 'Mood and the use of scripts,' *Journal of Personality and Social Psychology,* vol. (71) 1996, 665.

9. C. Haw, 'The family life cycle,' *Psychological Medicine,* vol. 25 (1995), 727.

10. R. Kean et al., 'Exploring factors of perceived social performance, health and personal control,' *International Journal of Aging and Human Development,* vol. 43 (1996), 297.

11. N. Ramanaiah et al., 'Sex role orientation and satisfaction with life,' *Psychological Reports,* vol. 71 (1995), 1260.

12. B. Fisher, 'Successful aging, life satisfaction and generativity in later life,' *International Journal of Aging and Human Development,* vol. 41 (1995), 239.

13. H. Lepper, 'In Pursuit of Happiness and Satisfaction in Later Life: A Study of Competing Theories of Subjective Well-being' (PhD thesis, University of California, Riverside, 1996).

14. N. Ramanaiah and F. Detwiler, 'Life satisfaction and the five model factor of personality,' *Psychological Reports,* vol. 80 (1997), 1208.

15. S. Hong and E. Giannakopoulos, 'Students' perceptions of life satisfaction,' *College Student Journal,* vol. 29 (1995), 438.

16. S. Rogers, 'Mothers' work hours and marital quality,' *Journal of Marriage and the Family,* vol. 58 (1996), 606.

17. E. Diener and F. Fujita, 'Resources, personal strivings and subjective well-being,' *Journal of Personality and Social Psychology,* vol. 68 (1995), 926.

18. S. Wilson et al., 'Life satisfaction among low income rural youth in Appalachia,' *Journal of Adolescence,* vol. 20 (1997), 443.

19. S. Bhargava, 'An integration-theoretical analysis of life satisfaction,' *Psychological Studies,* vol. 40 (1995), 170.

20. R. Smith, 'Experiencing Negative Effect' (master's dissertation, American University, Washington, 1997).

21. R. Bailey and C. Miller, 'Life satisfaction and life demands in college students,' *Social Behavior and Personality,* vol. 26 (1998), 51.

22. T. Gilovich and V. Medvec, 'Some counter factual determinants of satisfaction and regret,' in *What Might Have Been,* Mahway (NJ): Erlbaum 1995.

23. H. Lepper, 'In Pursuit of Happiness in Later Life: A Study in Competing Theories of Subjective Well-being' (PhD thesis, University of California, Riverside, 1996).

24. W. Pavot et al., 'The relation between self-aspect congruence, personality and subjective well-being,' *Personality and Individual Differences,* vol. 22 (1997), 183.

25. A. Furnham and H. Cheng, 'Personality and happiness,' *Psychological Reports,* vol. 80 (1997), 761.

26. C. Henry and S. Lovelace, 'Family resources and adolescent family satisfaction in remarried family households,' *Journal of Family Issues,* vol. 16 (1995), 1764.

27. M. Lindeman and M. Verkasalo, 'Meaning in life,' *Journal of Social Psychology,* vol. 136 (1996), 657.

28. M. Madigan et al., 'Life satisfaction and level of activity,' *Activities, Adaptation and Aging,* vol. 21 (1996), 21.

29. L. Lundqvist and U. Dimberg, 'Facial expressions are contagious,' *Journal of Psychophysiology,* vol. 9 (1995), 203.

30. H. Lepper, 'In Pursuit of Happiness and Satisfaction in Later Life: A Study of Competing Theories of Subjective Well-being' (PhD thesis, University of California, Riverside, 1996).

31. M. Sirgy et al., 'A life satisfaction measure,' *Social Indicators Research,* vol. 34, 236.

32. B. O'Connor, 'Family and friend relationships among older and younger adults,' *International Journal of Aging and Human Development,* vol. 40 (1995), 9, and M. Chand, 'An Inquiry into the Factors of Successful Marriages' (PhD thesis, Jadavpur University, Calcutta, 1990).

33. C. Notarius, 'Marriage: will I be happy or will I be sad?,' in *A Life Time of Relationships,* Pacific Grove (Calif.): Brooks-Cole, 1996.

34. R. Simpson, 'Conflict styles and social network relations as predictors of marital happiness' (PhD thesis, University of Michigan, Ann Arbor, 1990).

35. P. Ferroni and J. Taffee, 'Women's emotional wellbeing,' *Sexual and Marital Therapy,* vol. 12 (1997), 127.

36. C. Turner, 'Follow through conflict resolution as a factor in marital satisfaction and personal happiness' (master's dissertation, University of Nevada, Las Vegas, 1994).

37. K. Takahashi et al., 'Patterns of social relationships and psychological well-being among the elderly,' *International Journal of Behavioural Development,* vol. 21 (1997), 417.

38. F. Neto, 'Predictors of satisfaction with life,' *Social Indicators Research,* vol. 35 (93), 1995.

39. B. O'Connor, 'Family and friend relationships among older and younger adults,' *International Journal of Aging and Human Development,* vol. 40 (1995), 9.

40. V. B. Scott and W. D. McIntosh, 'The development of a trait measure of ruminative thought,' *Personality and Individual Differences,* vol. 26 (1999), 1045.

41. L. Li et al., 'The relationship between objective life status and subjective life satisfaction with quality of life,' *Behavioural Medicine,* vol. 23 (1998), 149.

42. M. Crist-Houran, 'Efficacy of volunteerism,' *Psychological Reports,* vol. 79 (1996), 736.

43. A. Williams et al., 'Altruistic activity,' *Activities, Adaptation and Aging,* vol. 22 (1998), 31, and L. Pegalis, 'Frequency and Duration of Positive Affect: The Dispositionality of Happiness' (PhD thesis, University of Georgia, Athens, Georgia, 1994).

44. Y. Jou and H. Fukada, 'Stress and social support in mental and physical health,' *Psychological Reports,* vol. 81 (1997), 1303.

45. J. Finch et al., 'The factor structure of received social support: dimensionality and the prediction of depression and life satisfaction,' *Journal of Social and Clinical Psychology,* vol. 16 (1997), 323.

46. K. Heatey and D. Thombs, 'Fruit vegetable consumption self-efficacy in youth,' *American Journal of Health Behavior,* vol. 21 (1997), 172.

47. P. Fontane, 'Exercise, fitness and feeling well,' *American Behavior Scientist,* vol. 39 (1996), 288.

48. J. Pilcher and E. Ott, 'The relationship between sleep and measures of health and well-being in college students: a repeated measures approach,' *Behavioral Medicine,* vol. 23 (1996), 170.

49. O. Alaoui-Ismaielie et al., 'Basic emotions evoked by odorants,' *Physiology and Behavior,* vol. 62 (1997), 713.

50. C. Murray and M. J. Peacock, 'A model free approach to the study of objective well-being,' *Mental Health in Black America,* Thousand Oaks (Calif.): Sage 1996.

51. Z. Magen et al., 'Experiencing joy and sorrow,' *International Forum of Logotherapy,* vol. 19 (1996), 45.

52. S. Sugarman, 'Happiness and population density' (master's dissertation, California State University, Long Beach, 1997).

53. M. Chand, 'An Inquiry into the Factors of a Successful Marriage' (PhD thesis, Jadavpur University, Calcutta, 1990).

54. L. Barofsky and A. Rowman, *Models of Measuring Quality of Life: Implications for Human Animal Interaction Research in Companion Animals in Human Health,* Thousand Oaks (Calif.): Sage 1998.

55. E. Hakanen, 'Emotional use of music by African American adolescents,' *Howard Journal of Communications,* vol. 5 (1995), 124.

56. T. Rahman and A. Khaleque, 'The purpose in life and academic behavior of problem students,' *Social Indicators Research,* vol. 39 (1996), 59.

57. D. Myers and A. Diener, 'Who is happy?,' *Psychological Science,* vol. 6 (1995), 10.

58. M. Botwin et al., 'Personality and mate preferences,' *Journal of Personality,* vol. 65 (1997), 107.

59. K. Panos, 'An exploration of related constructs and effects on happiness' (master's dissertation, American University, Washington, 1997).

60. J. Brown and K. Dutton, 'The thrill of victory, the complexity of defeat: self-esteem and people's emotional reaction to success and failure,' *Journal of Personality and Social Psychology,* vol. 68 (1995), 712.

61. M. Hunter and K. L. Liao, 'Problem solving groups for middle aged women in general practice,' *Journal of Reproductive and Infant Psychology,* vol. 13 (1995), 147.

62. J. Gerwood et al., 'The purpose in life test and religious denomination,' *Journal of Clinical Psychology,* vol. 54, 49.

63. I. Lipkus et al., 'The importance of distinguishing the belief in a just world for self versus others,' *Personality and Social Psychology Bulletin,* vol. 22, 666.

64. R. Garret, 'Wisdom as the key to a better world,' in *Contemporary Issues in Behaviour Therapy,* New York: Plenum 1996.

65. W. Oates, 'Reconciling with unfulfilled dreams at the end of life,' in *The Aging Family,* New York: Brunner-Mazel, 1997.

66. J. Brebner et al., 'Relationships between happiness and personality,' *Personality and Individual Differences,* vol. 19 (1995), 251.

67. S. Staats et al., 'Student well-being: are they better off now?,' *Social Indicators Research,* vol. 34, 93, and N. Chen, 'Individual Differences in Answering the Four Questions for Happiness' (PhD thesis, University of Georgia, Athens, Georgia, 1996).

68. J. Glass et al., 'Satisfaction in later life,' *Educational Gerontology,* vol. 23 (1997), 297.

69. D. Kehn, 'Predictors of elderly happiness activities,' *Adaptation and Aging,* vol. 19 (1995), 11.

70. D. Field, 'Looking back: what period of your life brought you the most satisfaction?,' *International Journal of Aging and Human Development,* vol. 45 (1997), 169.

71. J. Solomon, 'Humor and aging well,' *American Behavior Scientist,* vol. 39 (1996), 249, and H. Lepper, 'In Pursuit of Happiness and

Satisfaction in Later Life: A Study of Competing Theories of Subjective Well-being' (PhD thesis, University of California, Riverside, 1996).

72. E. Suh et al., 'Events and subjective well-being: only recent events matter,' *Journal of Personality and Social Psychology,* vol. 70, 1091.

73. E. Diener and M. Diener, 'Cross-cultural correlates of life satisfaction and self-esteem,' *Journal of Personality and Social Psychology,* vol. 68 (1995), 653.